The Absence of Death

Jack Moody

Copyright © 2024 Jack Moody

Cover by Cody Sexton of Anxiety Driven Graphics
Edited by Cassie Premo Steel, author of *Beaver Girl*
Formatted/designed by Paige Johnson, Outcast Press EIC

www.Outcast-Press.com

(e-book) ASIN: B0D6RM2DZK

(print) ISBN-13: 978-1-960882-13-4

For my family: Roxanne, Percy, and Theo

Author's Note

Each of these stories was originally published in different literary journals before becoming the book you have now in your hands, as denoted in the table of contents. Thanks to each.

I began writing these stories in September of 2021—the first, "Theo's Masterpiece," written immediately after I quit alcohol for the final time. I was frightened I would have no ability to write, nor anything to write about without alcohol. Luckily, that was not the case.

Nevertheless, quitting something I had been so reliant on for so long sent me into a place of severe isolation; I didn't know how else to keep from taking another drink. Born from that isolation was the inevitable retreat into my mind, dwelling upon the realization that I had come very, very close to death. I channeled that insight and fear and uncertainty into these 16 stories, completed over the next 14 months.

Writing this book was the reason I remained sober. So, for that, I'm thankful. Writing has saved my life in more ways than one. Have I come to terms with death?

No. I may never. But it's my hope that this book created in isolation can bring some sense of connection to someone who may be in the same dark depths that I was. In the end, that would mean more to me than any reconciliation with my mortality. In fact, that may be the only answer I found.

— Jack

Praise for Death

"A trippy kaleidoscope showcasing a universe of fallen human angels walking a precarious line between life and death, moving between the material world and visions, myth and hallucinations. Read it and let the words wash through your mortal being, your mind, your spirit. These stories will haunt you."

--Monica Drake, author of *Clown Girl* and *The Folly of Loving Life*

"Moody takes us through a collection of introspective, creative, and conceptual scenarios of life and death— especially the in-between. He brings us stories of the many ways people are *living to die* and *dying to live,* with a range from dementia, serial killings, cancer, the Garden of Eden with that treacherous fruit—to victims of pedophilic priests looking for retribution, hunters of people on the cusp of dying for that forbidden knowledge of the afterlife, aliens and much more. A lot of interesting sci-fi qualities to the pictures Jack likes to thoroughly paint. His work shines brightest when he balances the descriptive with his dope grasp of dialogue, which he is one of the best at."

---DuVay Knox, author of *The Pussy Detective* and *Soul Collector*

"Featuring the visceral language of the grotesque, mind-fuck aspects of the uncanny and injections of the absurd, *Absence*

of Death showcases Jack Moody's astonishing range. Moody firmly orients the reader in disorienting unrealities through graphic prose, veracious dialogue, and compelling characters. These death-heavy stories occupy hazy spaces between life and afterlife, forcing the reader to grapple with their own mortality and the consequences of living. Trippy, unsettling and surprising, this is a multi-genre compendium of lost souls languishing in limbo. And only a writer who has been on the brink himself can write from the bleakly beautiful, otherworldly place that Moody does."

--HLR, author of *History of Present Complaint* and *EX-CETERA*

"Hope you packed a lifejacket because the anchor just dropped, the rifles are loaded, and Moody's about to storm the beach. Read carefully. Stay close. This is what you trained for..."

--Scott Laudati, author of *Play the Devil* and *Bone House*

"Asimov, Serling, P.K. Dick, Matheson and Bradbury, Harlan Ellison and Octavia Butler plumbed the depths of human experience. These master fantasists understood compact narratives hold unique powers. Their verbal tableaus exposed us not only to supernatural mysteries, but experiential links that bind us to one another. Soon we will add a new name to that list: JACK MOODY."

--Jacob Ian DeCoursey, author of *Vivid Greene*

T

The Absence of Death

9

Originally published in
A Thin Slice of Anxiety

A

Carrying Eden

14

Originally published in
The Bel Esprit Project

B

Theo's Masterpiece

24

Originally published in
A Thin Slice of Anxiety

L

The Room Between Dreams

31

Originally published in
Misery Tourism

E

Pink Elephants

39

Originally published in
Paper and Ink Magazine, Issue 17

Begotten

44

Originally published in
Maudlin House

O

The Funeral of Joshua Miller

53

Originally published in
Apocalypse Confidential

F

The Last Cowboy

64

Originally published in
A Thin Slice of Anxiety

The Artist

Originally published in
A Thin Slice of Anxiety   **67**

Worm Food

Originally published in
Laughing Ronin Press: Seppuku, Issue 5   **81**

The Utopian Mask

Originally published in
Maudlin House and *NoSleep Podcast*   **91**

The Greatest Show on Earth

Originally published in
Punk Noir Magazine   **105**

A Ticket For The Night Bus

Originally published in
Roi Faineant Press   **111**

Terminal Optimism

Originally published in
A Thin Slice of Anxiety   **125**

The Light At The End Of The World

Originally published in
A Thin Slice of Anxiety   **132**

Flowers Bloom in Bardo

Originally published in
Roi Faineant Press   **138**

C

O

N

T

E

N

T

S

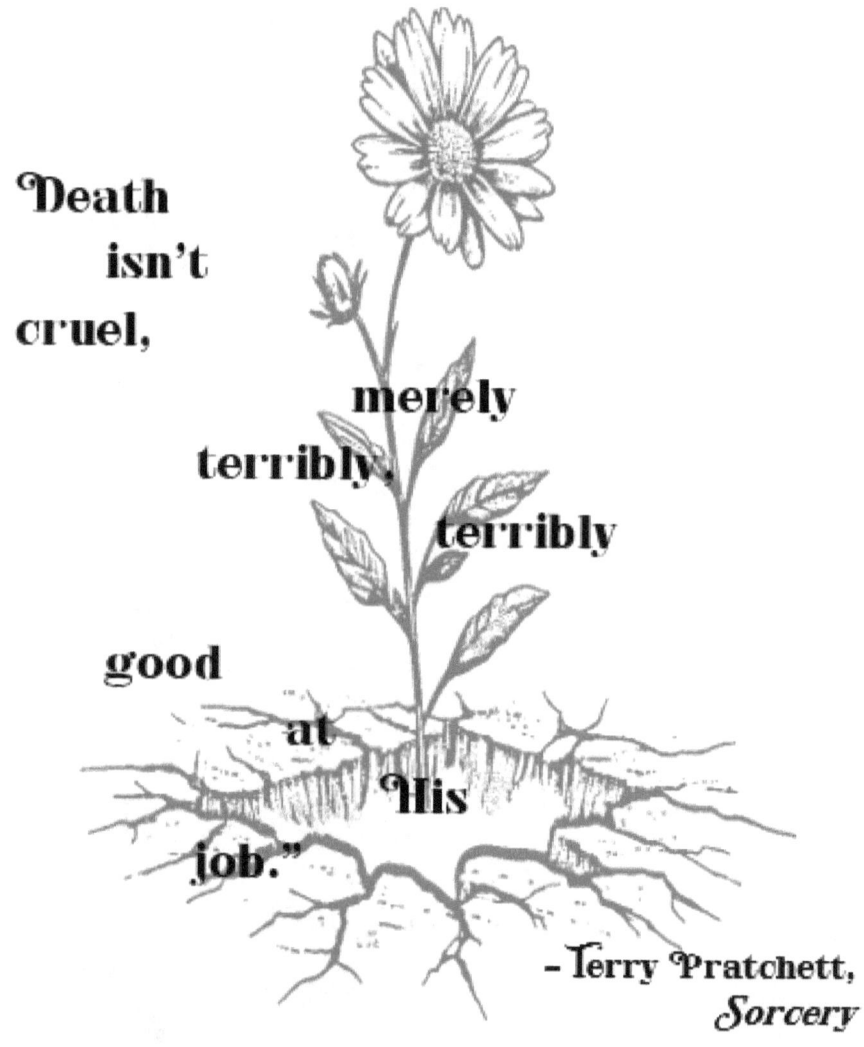

Death isn't cruel, merely terribly, terribly good at His job."

-Terry Pratchett, *Sorcery*

The Absence of Death

The moment it was introduced to his bloodstream, the process of dying had begun.

Breathing slowed to a hoarse whisper, the oxygen to his heart stalled, strangling the organ until the dirtied blood pumped like thick honey from a bottle. Body temperature rose, sweat began to pour from each gland. The brain suffocated, firing off neurons like weak explosives in the rain, drowning beneath the heavy flood of dopamine colliding with their outnumbered receptors. Fluids entered the blackened lung cavities and ejected as vomit and yellow foam, cascading forth from between the lips and down the chin.

In a final effort of comfort, the brain reached into its deepest memories and played for itself a movie called *Nostalgia*. And it watched all the wonderful things it had experienced in its life with her, as it slowly, slowly, slowly—went black.

The body was found and taken to a coroner, where he commented to a colleague while performing the autopsy, that if it weren't for the track marks and evidence of a tobacco addiction, he would have thought he was looking at a healthy young man.

The body was then placed in an incinerator, where it was burned for three hours at 1,800-degrees Fahrenheit, until the skin and flesh and fat and bone and muscle tissue became a large pile of gray ashes.

The pile of ashes was placed in an unmarked and ordinary metal container, and emptied into a collective grave, where it became part of an even larger pile of gray ashes and was promptly forgotten about.

This was when he woke up.

He walked for a long time. He crossed a bridge and past rows of buildings, and the lights of the city were there, and the people, too. They walked away and through him, and paid him no mind, nor did he them. Buildings became trees, and trees became forests, and, though he could no longer remember where he was, he continued to walk. The world moved as it always had, and this, and everything else, was no different than it had ever been.

He stopped beside a small creek and sat down with his knees to his chest, and watched the water move. It paid him no mind, and he was happy it allowed him to be there with it. There were too many places to look for her, and so much time had passed. He felt no rush to search. There was time, and there would always be time, and someday the time would stop but she wouldn't leave him.

He knew this.

Quiet was what he had taken for granted. And when he'd had it, it was beyond the veil, and it was meaningless. So, he remained by the creek, and they were quiet together until orange turned to blue, and the creek began to sparkle and gleam.

The city glowed in the distance, and the stars fizzled out within its reach, and he stood to return to the lights that choked out the sparkling quiet night, knowing that it did not have to be the last time he sat beside the creek in silence, but knew that, nevertheless, it would be.

As he delved deeper into the cracked, neon-lit streets, he returned to places he knew. These places at one time held significance but that feeling had withered, more and more with each place he found. The significance of them was how utterly insignificant they had become. Cravings were an alien concept. The sting, the warm familiarity of the act that had occurred within these places was of no consequence. He neither mourned nor celebrated this. It was now how it always would be, and there was nothing left in these places but the pockets of dust swept to and fro, forever unchanged, no different than it had ever been. They were empty, and hollow, and she was nowhere to be seen.

With only one final place to go, the place it had begun and would end, he made his way towards it, knowing if she hadn't returned to this place after all those passing days and nights, then she was gone for as long as time moved forward, until that too was finally gone, and only then could he find her again. This was all he had left for as long as the dust continued to be swept along with the rest of the world.

The streets had been a frightening and cold place without her body beside him, and they were dark and dirty, but the light she provided was the closest feeling to the warm sting he felt in those hollow buildings. Without her, fear was the way of the world, burnt into the yellow beams emanating from the swaying, shattered lamp posts, and impressed within the lungs taking air to fill the night with horrible, untended cries. It dripped from the open sores left to fester on the arms of the sick and untreatable. It exploded out with the snap of a hastily aimed gunshot.

With her, it was nothing but quiet.

She was the absence of death. He knew this.

He retraced the steps he'd taken a hundred times in a haze of delirium, the haze now lifted, acutely aware of the darting eyes of those who would never dare look as he crossed their paths.

A man and woman sat huddled on the sidewalk before the building, its dilapidated walls hardly any more protection from the elements than the brown-stained clump of charity blankets draped over their bodies. He paused to sit beside them, and, although they weren't people he knew, they were people he could have and would have known through opportunity or necessity.

"I've lived longer than I ever wanted to," the man said. "I've lived long enough. I'm cold. I'm too sick. I've had enough."

"A little longer then," said the woman. "Just a little longer. What am I supposed to do without you?"

"You'll have twice the blankets," the man said. "Twice the money. Twice the food. Twice the dope. You'll manage."

"But I'll still be twice as cold. Twice as poor. I won't eat. I'll be twice as hungry. I would rather share."

He turned and watched a group of people talking and laughing amongst themselves, wearing shiny dresses and dry-cleaned suits. They stopped long enough to eye the man and woman and speed up to cross the street.

They ignored the laughing people, as they always did, and the people did not turn around or stop, as they always would.

"You'll manage," the man repeated.

"We're better as a team," said the woman. "We're good to each other. You can't leave. I just won't let you."

The man shifted underneath the blankets and coughed. It rattled inside his chest and a glob of black phlegm followed, landing on the pavement. "Then I'll find you in the next one."

"Do you promise?" said the woman.

"Yes."

"How can you promise that?"

"I can see things," the man answered.

"What kind of things?"

"Good things." The man wrapped an arm around the woman as wind whipped across their faces. "I see good things."

"I can't fall asleep until you do," said the woman. She tucked herself deeper into the man's body, and pulled the blankets up to her chin, the scabs and broken veins no longer visible beneath her blue eyes. "Not until I hear you snoring."

"Then be quiet," the man said. "And I'll wake you in the morning."

He stood, leaving the man and woman to rest, and walked forward, through the boarded-up entrance to the building. The flood of acknowledgment and memory coursed through him as he stepped across the room. Discarded needles and bags of trash littered the floor, and the floorboards creaked and moaned in recognition of his return. The silvery, translucent forms of people he'd known sat crouched against the walls, hugging the corners and, though their eyes met, there was nothing left to say. They were only there to watch the pockets of dust, and to wait. What they were waiting for was something he would never know, because it was theirs, and until they found it, there they would remain. Until the dust cleared and time stopped.

He didn't see her among his old friends, and something that felt vaguely like—what must have been—fear flowed like shifting ice inside him. He made his way up the stairs, stepping around holes in the rotted wood and rusted nails, knowing there was nowhere left to search but the room he was about to enter. Otherwise, he would join the ranks of the lost and unclaimed drifting in the room below, and he too would sit and wait. For as long as it took, he would wait for her.

Thin beams of moonlight shone through the cracks in the ceiling, bathing the room in a blue film. In the corner was a single sleeping bag, upon it a puddle of yellow vomit that had dried and hardened. A layer of dust lined the sleeping bag and collapsing floor, though the pillow remained untouched. Strewn across the room were dozens of dead mice. Like watching the process of death fast-forwarded frame by frame, each body was in a different state of decay. Some had been reduced to skeletons, while others appeared freshly deceased, the streaks of blood coating their fur still shimmering crimson in the light.

He strained to believe he had merely missed her upon his first glimpse, his eyes scanning the floor, the empty walls and the corners collecting dust, over and over and over, waiting for the flash of her silhouette.

But she was gone.

The shifting ice returned inside him. He navigated between the graveyard of mice, sat down upon the stained sleeping bag, and accepted what was to come: the long wait. Piercing and consuming in its silence, not quiet. Not quiet, because she was gone.

Hours passed. Or months, or years, he waited. How long could no longer be measured and no longer mattered. The only metric that now existed was the moments before she had gone, and the single moment they would be reunited at the end.

Until something broke through the cacophony of silence.

A single noise. A familiar sound.

The soft cry followed softer footsteps, the aching wood muted beneath their tiny weight.

She appeared at the top of the stairs. Though her features had aged, and long, gray streaks adorned her once jet-black and heavy coat, he knew at once it was her. She stopped for a moment, frozen. In her eyes was the unmistakable awareness of him.

Stepping closer, she dropped a freshly killed mouse at the foot of the sleeping bag and began to purr. The sound drowned out the world. Her nose lifted into the air, and she began to circle him, pawing at nothing, but she knew, and her purrs grew louder and louder, until it encompassed his whole being, and the ice melted away.

He reached down closer to her, and saw she had been bathed, her coat shining and clean and full. Around her neck was a collar he had never seen. Dangling from it was a small metal tag and written upon that was a name he had never used.

She stepped onto the pillow beside him untouched by the dust, curled into a ball, and fell asleep, ever purring.

It became very quiet in the room.

He smiled. And at that moment, he disappeared from the Earth. He no longer had to wait. They each knew where to look. And they would find each other again at the end.

Carrying Eden

In the beginning, the skies created a torrent of light and sound. The world screamed and then bellowed, whipping the land like lashes upon a body. Lucy sat hunched at the edge of her open mouth of stone, staring up at the gray and undulating ceiling that had once been a pale blue canvas.

Though it was dark, she knew the violent argument overhead had not brought about those quiet hours where creatures called and roamed throughout the shadows of the brush. In those quiet hours where her eyelids grew heavy and beckoned her to the other world she would not remember, the pale blue canvas became a shimmering gradient of blue and black, dotted with bright, unblinking eyes.

The eyes would stand guard against the creatures in the brush, shining their light upon the darkest corners until the great red giant returned to welcome her back into the tangible world to which she was accustomed.

Lucy waited for its anger to pass, for its tantrum to cease, wide-eyed and curious, accepting that the other world wouldn't beckon with the skies so distracting and full of rage.

There were few times when the other world didn't beckon, and Lucy huddled inside the stone mouth, listening to unfamiliar cries in the darkness, her breath shallow and quickened, the thumps inside her chest injecting her limbs with the tingling urge to run or scream in return. Those quiet and sightless hours moved like honey through a hollowed stick, and she felt no hunger or thirst, and only wished for the unblinking eyes to ward off those who would harm her.

And each time, they did; for the great red giant would always arise from behind the faraway peaks, peeling away the shadows' fog, and the cries became songs of the winged creatures that flitted between the limbs of forest giants.

Lucy felt the heat of wrath with each crack of white light that struck the ground but could find no reason the skies would be angry with her. If the skies were in poor spirits, it had to be with another creature, another giant, some other being that had incurred its need for vengeance. She revered the unblinking eyes for protecting her while she traveled away inside her head and hoped that it wasn't they who were being punished. A world without their watchful glow during the quiet and dark hours was a world she couldn't bear to fathom.

Sometimes on those clear nights, Lucy would return the unblinking gaze, looking out at the entities she knew little about, but loved with such an intensity, it was as if they were the source of her existence. And so, she would speak to the eyes, asking questions to fill the quiet hours, and though they didn't respond as she did, they told her stories in the skies.

They created shapes resembling things she knew and regaled her with tales through the images. Tales of mighty heroes who conquered the creatures in the shadows, the celestial blood dripping from their weapons made from the eyes falling across the heavens until disappearing behind the veiled peaks. Tales of beings like her, beings she only knew to be similar because they shared the same form as what gazed back when she hunched down to drink from the streams.

These beings like her stood upright, proud and unafraid, and their form was illuminated by the medium their creators painted. They traveled vast distances and built beautiful things that bloomed within their minds as they visited their other world. They spread across the sky like the tiny creatures that emerged from their mounds of earth, multiplying far across the cosmos, taming beasts and the world alike, molding it to their liking.

The unblinking eyes revealed beings that shared Lucy's appearance, but their stories were unimaginable, their feats seemingly unattainable, and so she couldn't believe she and they were of the same kind. They were something greater, something beyond. They were something she wished to know and become. The unblinking eyes showed Lucy what was possible. Beings born from the skies in her image, maternal and aspirational.
She didn't know what to call these beings, but believed them to be true, because the eyes had never once betrayed her. The eyes were showing from where she came: the womb of the world.

With terror controlling her mind, Lucy crawled out farther from her mouth of stone, and allowed the tears to fall from the skies upon her as the cracks of light struck. She knew nothing of what the argument meant, only that if the unblinking eyes were being suffocated behind the gray ceiling, she would never again feel the safety they created, never again watch the stories they told her of her past and future.

A world without illumination was an empty one, and one in which she could never continue.

And so, with no plan to speak of, she yelled out at the undulating, violent skies, calling for peace. She screamed for their anger to subside, for the womb of the world to open again, for the eyes to be revealed so they could breathe and brighten her darkened hours that would surely prove to be her demise.

Lucy screamed and screamed, filling her lungs with each outburst to stifle the mighty cracks of light like boulders hurled onto soft flesh. The skies' tears wetted her face, trying to overpower her voice, but still she thrust her own cries at the dark mass overhead, her feet planted into the earth as if in the heat of combat. The eyes had shown her what she was capable of, and Lucy refused to kowtow to the entity that would be their killer.

In a lapse between strikes, the skies relented just long enough for Lucy to unleash what was left of her strength, filling the brief static with a final war cry.

It left her body like a separate creature, galloping into the gray ceiling and spreading across the world in echoes that bore echoes, and the skies heard.

A moment of silence passed, the tears ceasing their assault, and from the armistice came a final monolithic strike like a serpent upon a mouse. It careened into the largest forest giant standing at the clearing's edge, and, in a brilliant eruption of light and sound, the giant fell.

Its death created a trench in the earth. And there before Lucy's eyes, from its sacrificial body was born a spark. It aged and grew, and in place of what was hidden, it became its own burning light. It was a child of the great red giant, glowing not in the pale skies, but upon the earth and the forest itself. The child was heat and safety and illumination in the dark.

The turbulent skies, impressed with Lucy's strength against an incalculable opponent, granted her their son—a sentry in the unblinking eyes' absence.

Lucy approached and dropped to her knees at the edge of its warming glow, thanking the skies that still bellowed and shifted. But with what they had given her, their will could be experienced without fear. For a son had been granted, and the son that flickered and tasted the air would remain atop the giant's body, and no creatures in the brush would dare approach and defy this gift from above. The son was the skies' anger and wrath contained, biting at the spaces beyond its reach, but remaining within its given post, just as no earthly son would ever go against his elders' strict command.

The son was of no creation Lucy had ever seen. It was unable to be grasped or conquered and coughed black wisps into the skies as it took on the same colors that preceded the great red giant when it rose from the peaks each day. Though it would protect her, the son frightened Lucy, and she felt herself instinctively recoiling from its gaze as it hacked and spit and shape-shifted atop the forest giant's corpse.

There was no camaraderie shared like there was with the unblinking eyes, and so she chose to leave the son to its given duty, retreating into the mouth of stone to visit her other world where perhaps the eyes waited.

Despite her trepidation with the entity bestowed by the skies, she knew it would not waver, and she was safe from the creatures in the brush. For that, she thanked the son, but decided to never try to speak to it again. Within its slithering form was chaos. And chaos was her demise if it were to be a friend.

From inside her mouth of stone, Lucy heard a great hum. Its melody urged her to wake, like a weeping spirit, calling her towards an unfamiliar radiance. She stood, seeing that it was still the quiet hours, but something was different. In the clearing, there was a wide beam of light. And within the beam, where the sentry had stood flickering atop the forest giant's body, was a new being, a new forest giant whose appearance and magnitude was unlike anything she'd ever witnessed.

Stepping into the clearing, Lucy stared up in awe. The being was taller than a mountain, rising far above where the gray ceiling had held dominance. Its limbs stretched out across the world in all directions, the leaves they bore harbored every color to exist. Like embryos of the giant, they bloomed out of one another, erupting into bushels of greens and blues and reds and purples, becoming alive as the massive roots crawled out across the earth like the tendrils of a sea monster.

But despite the giant's stature, the encompassing beam seemed to magnify and warp its hum into a peaceful lullaby. The forest giant was singing through vibrations and color.

Lucy approached, reaching a tentative hand inside the beam to stroke the being's trunk.

The light dissolved inside her skin, ballooning within her, and she felt the presence of what the unblinking eyes had shown her each night. Lucy craned her neck to the skies, peering through the kaleidoscope of flora, and saw in the glimpses of night that the eyes had returned, joining with the glow to bathe the darkened world in illumination. The beam reached down from the heavens, under their watchful gaze, a conduit from their world to Lucy's, and she saw the images they created moving across the canvas: the greater beings like her that seemed so much less out of reach with the forest giant closing the gap between their two realities.

Then something else captured Lucy's attention. It hung from the highest limb that pierced the night's canopy, shrouded in magenta foliage and imbued with glittering light. It was a perfectly round, plump and ripe fruit, the shade of fresh blood drawn from a kill. It was so far away, so out of reach, but Lucy wanted what the giant had borne, and knew it was for her.

The soft hum grew and grew, swelling into a hypnotic mantra, asking Lucy to take of the fruit, to find a way to reach the top of the world. It begged of her to become what the unblinking eyes had revealed, to become what was possible, to tap into the furthest reaches of her potential, and to greet the beings in the skies as an equal. All it would take was to pluck the fruit from the giant's peak.

Lucy knew that she couldn't do this alone, and so dug her hands into the soft earth that surrounded the being and began to build. Instinct drove her forward as she formed the clay into the image of what glowed within her mind, and she severed the lowest hanging limbs as sacrifice for her creation.

Soon they became great limbs like her own, sealed to the clay and earth that became flesh, and under the light of the murmuring beam, life was slowly exhaled into the massive creature she built. She packed on more and more clay, the compiled earth heaving as it began to breathe and take in air on its own. Under the unblinking eyes, she toiled, cocooned by the falling leaves that blanketed the ground and melted into her creation's form as muscle and bone and organs.

The skies glittered purple, the world reflecting her excitement; brilliant and vibrant and real, and Lucy stepped away to look upon what she'd done and saw that it was good.

She came to the nearby creek to retrieve two stones and returned to the head of the enormous mirror in her likeness and placed the stones in hand-carved pockets.

The great beam exhaled again, and the stones blinked and looked at their creator, and the being stood up.

It stretched over the forest giant, and looked upon the world, the place of its birth, and looked down upon Lucy, its mother. It ran its hands through the colorful leaves, shaking loose whole branches that fell at Lucy's feet, and gazed up at the unblinking eyes, their images a mirror of what it was and would be.

Lucy called up to her child and asked it to retrieve the fruit from the highest limb, and to bring it back for her to taste—a gift to its mother as thanks for its newly given life.

Her child did as it was asked, retrieving the fruit, and bent down as low as it could, a mountain contorting its shape, laying its hand down upon the earth. Lucy stepped onto her child's palm and picked up the fruit that was like a speck of dust attached to the creature's clay flesh.

She thanked her child, and it stared at her with its tiny, obsidian stone eyes, and rose back to its full height to commune with the images in the skies.

The fruit was more perfect in her hand than she could ever imagine. Its scent arose and intertwined with the forest giant, blooming more and more leaves that whistled as the beam hummed and murmured and glowed.

She held infinite possibility. She held paradise.

Lucy took a bite of the fruit. But what she tasted was not sweet. It was not filling, nor satisfying. It tasted like no paradise she'd ever conceive. When Lucy ate of the fruit, she tasted exactly what was presented when she saw it hanging from the unreachable limb.

Lucy tasted blood.

She spit out the fruit like bile after swallowing rotten meat, and its juices ran down her chin, and the juices stung and burned, and at once the skies became the undulating, gray ceiling she remembered, and the bellows followed screams that tore away the glowing beam, and, with it, disappeared the great hum, and tears again fell from the skies.

Lucy looked up at her child and saw in horror that its likeness to her had withered into a sickening monstrosity, a warped mirror of her corpse, defiled and fly-bitten and decomposed. Pieces of clay rained down upon the earth as her child crumbled, finding the tears as they together fell, and from their new marriage of anger and fear and decay came a mudslide that knocked Lucy off her feet, and, as the remains of her dead child swept her away from the forest giant, she saw born from the skies a single thunderous strike of light that lashed its body like splitting open a ribcage.

The giant that was once vibrant and massive and beautiful toppled under the weight of the skies' rage, and a spark formed atop its fallen corpse as it crashed to the earth with the force of an apocalypse, and a son of the great red giant spread and engulfed it and the forest under its dominion.

As Lucy was pulled beneath the mud and rapids, the last thing she witnessed was a sea of death before the water's surface, and flames became the ceiling of her tomb.

When Lucy awoke from the other world, she screamed until her ears rang. Outside the mouth of stone, light seeped in from the great red giant hanging above faraway peaks. The skies were again a pale blue canvas. The argument had passed.

She emerged into the clearing, the brightness of day forcing her eyes to squint, and saw the body of the felled forest giant. Upon it were the dying embers of the skies' gift, still hissing and caked in a bed of black ashes. A microcosm of small creatures adorned the giant's remains, darting through hollows and feasting upon what was left to salvage. The songs of winged creatures blew through the leaves with the wind, and the world was a calm and peaceful place.

The events that had occurred in the other world were sinking into the unknowable depths of her mind, disintegrating like dust in water as she combed through the images, knowing something far below cried out for remembrance, but its cries were distant and in vain, as they slinked through the cracks of her fleeting recollection and disappeared.

All Lucy understood was that an irreparable hole had been carved into her. She felt the beauty of the natural world around her funneling into the hole, the oxygen and vibrancy snuffed as their essence was swallowed. There was a space inside her that drained life and filtered it into a dread she had never felt. It wasn't a fear of the dark and quiet hours, or the creatures in the brush, or the absence of the unblinking eyes; it was the ever-looming and intangible result of what these things all represented—of what had never been a concept she could fathom.

The dread took form as a heavy, spectral hand on her shoulder, and the hand squeezed and constricted her thoughts into a narrow tunnel, and all that could be seen, despite her recognition of the wondrous existence unfurled before her, was the dim end of the tunnel that had commandeered her awareness:

Lucy was going to die.

In the expiring embers of the great red giant's son, Lucy saw inescapable Fate. Mortality emerged from the ashes, its grip sliding from her shoulder to reach out and greet her as a friend. Its image was a horror incomprehensible, lucid and void of form, but with the hulking presence of the skies themselves. It was the hole inside her, eating away at the present. It was within her, and had always been, gnawing through the center until revealing itself like a maggot burrowing to the surface of a decomposing animal.

In disgust, Lucy turned away, refusing to look at what had already taken hold, her eyes frantically scanning the skies and forest and creatures, anything that would pull her from underneath the weight of her revelation.

But the world was draining of color, and purpose, and certainty, and all she could see was what it would become: the skies black and devoid of sight, the giants felled, the creatures prone and motionless. All that would remain were the ashes and the hissing embers, until fire and soot was the resting place of her own body, her mind evaporated and lost with the water that had filled the now silent, empty creek.

And still, Mortality held out its hand, waiting.

Lucy escaped towards the giant's body, running her hand against its cold and hard skin, desperately searching for a glimmer of life, but the creatures all fled deeper into the forest's shadows, and the leaves fell and crumbled beneath her touch. Still, she searched, unwilling to cry out, unwilling to speak to the skies that had lied to her, that had killed or hidden away the unblinking eyes; those ephemeral raconteurs had showed her hope and solace in the face of terror. Still, she searched, because she was alone with the inevitable, and no answer would be found but the one she'd discover on her own, because nothing else could be trusted but her intuition. Her mind was corrupted, her perception untrustworthy. Forever damaged by the knowledge never requested.

She came to the giant's head, Mortality's specter breathing down her neck. What were once grand and bountiful limbs had been picked clean and desecrated—except one.

Attached to what had been the highest limb of all, now limp upon the ground but untouched, was a solitary ripe fruit.

It was the image of life and vibrancy: Bright. Vivid. Plump. Blood red.

A sliver of untarnished birth hidden in the swamp of decay.

Lucy reached down to pluck the fruit from its splintered stem, and saw that even the tiniest creatures, patrolling in a long line towards their mound of earth with spoils atop their backs, made a wide arch in their route to avoid the object.

Nothing at all had touched it: There were no punctures, no bites taken, no skin torn, pulp spilled. It was immaculate. It was perfect. It was her answer.

It had to be.

Holding the fruit in her palm, Lucy felt its essence like a vibration throughout her bones, and it hummed with a song that reminded her of a place far away. Something about it, though, was wrong, as if it had come from another realm and was placed in her world as a fraudulent beacon to fulfill some larger puzzle. It didn't fit.

Lucy felt the grip of Mortality's hand again on her shoulder. Its breath was cold on her neck like a stinging winter breeze, raising the hairs on her nape. Before she could recoil at its touch, Mortality wrapped itself around her like a burial shroud, and her mind slowed, and the tunnel narrowed, and the dim light at its end grew bright.

"What do you see?" it whispered into her ear. "Tell me what you see."

Lucy squeezed her eyes shut, focusing on the alien perfection of the fruit whose hum had become an alluring invitation.

When she refused to respond, Mortality whispered, "Do you want to make it stop? I can make the journey easier. I can dim the light. Do you want that?"

Lucy relaxed her muscles, and Mortality's embrace grew tighter.

"I can give you what you want. That which exists in the skies—what you watch every night. What you yearn for. I can give it to you."

The tunnel of her mind became filled with the glittering night sky, the beings and mighty heroes in her likeness dancing and calling for her to be their creator. To give them life. To free them from the skies and bring them to the world. To be her answer.

Mortality's lips were now against her ear, orgasmic yet frigid. "*All you have to do*—"

Lucy placed the fruit in her mouth, and ate.

Theo's Masterpiece

Theo awoke upon soft earth. He lifted his head with the difficulty of one coming from a deep but restless slumber, and he wiped the granules stuck to his face by the drool that had pooled underneath his cheek. From his prone vantage point, he could make out the trunks of trees like elephants' legs, and between them grew many patches of pale-yellow flowers.

Upon standing, a bout of dizziness struck Theo. The air was so thick with humidity, he found it difficult to fill his lungs. The dense forest shadowed his direct line of sight though, when he craned his neck towards the sky, he could see the pale blue, cloudless blanket overhead and followed the thin rays that reached through the canopy in sparse pockets.

Theo remembered hearing once—what felt like a lifetime ago—that when lost in the wilderness, one should seek out running water. One can then follow the current back to safety. With no other survival tips rattling around his memories, Theo closed his eyes, spun in circles on his heels, and stopped. What lay in front of him appeared no different in any other direction, and so he decided this direction was where he would go.

As he traversed through berry bushes and grass that stood up to his neck, and over boulders and fallen trees, a few things slowly became apparent: This forest was devoid of sound. There was no whistling of the wind through the leaves, nor birdcalls, nor chattering animals skittering across the ground. There were only the sounds of his soft footsteps and the silence so great that it almost had a voice of its own. Theo too noticed that the light from the sky hadn't waxed nor waned. It was like looking up at a solid, unchanging shade of cerulean thinly spread over the canopy like Saran wrap.

As hard as he tried to catch a glimpse of the sun through the treetops, there was nothing. The daylight seemed to come from no tangible source. It was as if time was in a standstill. Lastly, and most peculiar of all, becoming more unsettling as he traveled on, was that everything around him—the bark of the trees, the leaves, the bushes, the boulders, the grass and the earth beneath his feet, even the sky's shade of blue—all appeared dull, almost lifeless, as if the color of the world and everything in it had been drained. It was like seeing through fogged glasses or being struck with a vague form of color blindness. Nevertheless, Theo continued, forced to set these odd phenomena aside until he could find running water. It wouldn't do to dwell on anything yet but his need to escape.

It wasn't until exhaustion began to overtake him, did Theo finally catch the first sign of freedom. After climbing down a short cliff face, he sensed it just on the other side of the treeline a few yards ahead: the smell of water. Though there was no sound of a current, it reached his nostrils as clear as could be. The cooling, refreshing sensation of lifeblood was close. With no other sensory stimuli available, the acute instinct that water was nearby became overpowering. It was like feeling a weak pulse in a dying body.

Newly invigorated, Theo began to run, his body aching for a drink. He pushed through the dense underbrush, and, upon reaching the edge of the clearing, found what he'd been looking for. Theo then stood at the bank of a great snaking river cutting down the middle of an open field and into the woods at either direction. He kneeled and reached a trembling hand into the water and froze in confusion. Though the water was cool, he felt nothing but stagnation. The river was still, and like everything else he'd found, a pale, murky reflection of the sky above. It was as if the current was frozen in time.

"Hello."

After such a time hearing nothing but silence, the sound of another person's voice fired a sharp wave of fear up and down his body. Theo's head shot up and turned over his shoulder.

Standing at the edge of the treeline was a man. Another living person. "Hello there," the man repeated, leaning against one of the enormous trunks. "Lost?"

Theo stood, peering shrewdly at the man, unable to tell if this was a hallucination.

He had a childlike face, a layer of youthful fat hiding the definition that comes in adulthood, but his skin was weathered, and his eyes were a bright and knowing green, the first burst of real color Theo had seen since awakening in this place. He wore a cloak of pure white, seemingly untouched by the dirt and brush of the woods.

After a moment of hesitancy, Theo relinquished the words, "Yes. Yes, I think so. Do you know where we are?"

The man smiled and stepped closer. "Well, we're here. I'd thought that would be obvious." Before Theo could respond to his frustrating answer, the man approached beside him at the riverbank and sat down cross-legged. "Do you remember where you were before you came here? I often find that recalling where *there* is helps me know where *here* is."

Theo was about to snap at the man for talking in riddles, when the words caused him to pause. "I..." Theo started, his mind searching as he looked around at his surroundings as though they would provide his answer. "I don't know. I can't remember where I was before." The terror of this realization set in like a stone sinking to the bottom of his stomach. He hadn't thought about the events before his awakening. There was nothing before this. All he knew was being in the forest. How long had he been here?

The man looked up at Theo and frowned. "That's a pity. With no 'there,' it's always difficult to find 'here.' But not impossible. Why don't you sit?"

Theo complied, resting upon the earth next to the man as he reached a wrinkled hand into the stagnant river. "Odd, isn't it?" the man said, watching the water spill between his fingers. "Funny what the mind can do. Well, I can't tell you why you're here. Only you can know that. But in a dull and still world, the fact that you're the only thing with any life says something. What it says, though, I don't quite know. But it's talking."

"What about you?" Theo asked, turning to the man.

He smiled. "What about me?"

Theo didn't feel like pressing the odd stranger, as it was becoming clear he wouldn't provide any information that didn't require mental gymnastics. He stared into the glimmering river, gazing through the surface at the bed of clay. "I just want to go home. Where does this river g—"

"Perhaps you are home," the man interrupted. "Anything is possible. It just may not look very much like home yet. But it's funny what the mind can do. Life, and even death, is only what we make of it. Something to think about."

Theo, growing angry with the games, hissed, "Look, old man—"

But when he turned to face him, the man was gone.

Theo remained at the river's edge for some time. No longer consumed with the immediate need to escape the woods, his mind had become transfixed by the ephemeral man and his words. Though he believed that what the old man had told him held some key to the nature of his predicament, Theo couldn't make sense of what door it may open. His reality was becoming more intangible the longer he took stock. It was as though he'd been shaken from the throes of a very convincing dream.

He considered that he was merely becoming lucid in the most lifelike dream state his mind had ever conjured. This didn't quite feel correct, but he compartmentalized his trepidation and chose to find some comfort in the possibility that all this was occurring in his mind as his physical body peacefully slumbered on his bed. But the further he followed his thoughts down this line of reasoning, the more confused he became. There was no memory of a bed, or a home, or a life at all. Theo was operating with the self-awareness and recollection of a newborn.

Theo stood, toying with the old man's words, letting them tumble between the corners of his mind. He looked at the bleak sky. He wanted the light of the stars, the glow of the moon, the deep blue of night to comfort him like the safety of a locked room.

Suddenly, as the thoughts echoed inside his head, something fantastic happened. Theo no longer felt the solid ground beneath his feet. He looked down and, with no twinge of fear, saw the earth shrinking away from him. Floating up and up and up like a discarded balloon, Theo saw the trees like elephant limbs become children's figurines. The river like a dead serpent went on beyond the horizon, as devoid of vitality as the rest of the world he could see with clear eyes. The great expanse of dulled flora became one large gray organism, like blood-drained skin stretched loosely over the body of a once gorgeous creature on its deathbed. The artificial-blue sky he now touched resembled the sterile fluorescence of a hospital room.

Theo's reality shifted again. The idea that what he was about to do had never occurred to him felt laughable and naive. He would paint the sky. He would paint the earth. He would paint the trees and the wind and the current. Theo would give his world a pulse.

Theo lifted himself higher in the air, until the world below was a vague blur. He lifted an arm over his head, and, with focus like Michelangelo looking at the Sistine Chapel ceiling, he waved his palm across the sky. As his hand passed over his canvas, what was the stark shade of grayish-cerulean became alive—a deep, full, navy blue blanketed the earth. Night fell across the sky at his command, like the goddess Selene flying through the heavens in her chariot.

Content with what he'd created, Theo flexed his fingers as if flicking off droplets, and a dazzling burst of constellations lit up a corner of the midnight air. Again and again, he did this until the celestial bodies bathed the gray forest with golden light. Carefully, he pointed an index finger at an empty blue pocket and traced the outline of a crescent moon. After connecting the outline, it appeared, beaming a fantastic and reflective yellow. Theo felt the sudden chill of a light breeze passing through, ruffling his hair and cooling his sweating brow. The pulse of his world was becoming stronger.

Overwhelmed with excitement, Theo dove down through his creation until landing softly back upon the gray earth. He looked around at the sickly woods. The possibilities were almost too much to fathom. Movement—he wanted movement, he wanted life. Leaning down on one knee, Theo dipped his hand into the stagnant river, and, with a forceful motion, pushed the water forward as if telling it to return to its natural state. A heavy current pushed with him, down the length of the carved bed of clay. He cupped his hand and brought it to his mouth, drinking deep from the water until it spilled down his chin. He could feel his heartrate increasing. The exhaustion from his travels and the humidity drained from his body like a great weight.

Theo looked upward to appreciate his work. It was only right that the earth below should match the heavens in colorful brilliance. He reached his hand into the river once more, feeling the rapid movement of water and listening to the noise it created like a symphony of static. Like someone had dumped a bucket of oil paint, the water turned a luminescent gold, lighting up the edges of the forest all the way down like candle lampposts. His changing world had showed him his path.

Swaying his hands to and fro like an orchestra conductor as he walked, the leaves of the trees all around him burst into radiant oranges and reds and greens, glittering as if a great swarm of fireflies were hovering amongst the branches. With each step taken, patches of kaleidoscopic flowers erupted out from the ground in his wake.

Theo's surroundings began to take on the appearance of thousands of paintbrush strokes, less a natural reality but a surrealist piece of artwork. The ground undulated like he was standing atop an ocean, and he experienced the distantly familiar sensation of resting upon the chest of a breathing, living being.

WE'VE GOT SOMETHING.

Theo stopped in his path. He looked up and around and behind him. He was sure he heard the words, disconnected and ethereal, as if carried by the wind, but couldn't find a person to which the voice was attached.

GET THEM OUTTA THE ROOM.

The shimmering colors in the trees and the glow of the golden river began rhythmically fading in and out like blinking traffic lights, and the ground shook and vibrated as if an earthquake had struck. Something farther down the path appeared: such a bright and intense white light that Theo had to hold a hand to his eyes. It was the source of the voice. He could hear the words more clearly the closer he got.

Theo took off into a sprint towards the apparition, as the tremors of the woods grew into such intensity that he could hardly keep his footing.

STAY WITH ME, THEO. STAY WITH ME.

The disembodied voice exploded with the booming, omnipotent force of a god. Theo's lungs burned, the light ahead so powerful, he squeezed his eyes shut, only following the words' increasing volume. Flowers burst forth beneath his footsteps, pushing out and against his soles as if urging him forward.

Then, all at once, like turning off the light in a room, everything ceased. The ground settled, the erratic blinking of his world sank back into a soft incandescence, and Theo stopped. He felt the warm glow of something just beyond reach. The only sound echoing through the wind was a steady and rhythmic electronic beep.

Theo opened his eyes.

He'd reached the apparition. A rectangle of white light stood alone in the woods before him. It was a door.

Theo felt a hand on his shoulder.

He turned around, and there beside him was the old man.

Without a word, the man smiled and nodded, stepped forward into the door, and disappeared.

Come back to us, Theo.

The voice floated over to him from beyond the light.

Come back.

Theo took a tentative step, and his foot dissolved into the illuminated void. He breathed in deep, looked at the burning blue sky, at the world he brought to life, and walked through the door.

Theo awoke to the face of a man in a surgical mask staring down at him. "We almost lost you there," he said. "Welcome back, Theo."

The Room Between Dreams

❋   I.

Abner awoke from a wonderful dream. Sunlight poured into his room, the unadorned white walls reflecting the sun's rays like layers of snow. He squeezed his eyes shut, focusing on the images that had played in his mind, reaching for the remnants before they dissolved behind his waking life: a beach with golden sand, a young woman in a pink-striped bathing suit, a boy and girl laughing in the shade beneath a leaning umbrella. He strained to put together their features before the faces melted away into a gray blanket of static.

On the bedside table were a glass of water and a piece of paper. He reached for the glass and put it to his lips, letting the water sit on his tongue before swallowing. It was cold and dry in the room, and his skin felt taut, yet it stung when his hand stroked the deep wrinkles on his cheek.

Abner detested the brightness of early morning. There were no mirrors in his room, but under the unavoidable lightness of day, the liver spots and spider veins decorating the backs of his hands became glaring and disturbingly vivid. He had taken good care of himself, or he had tried to, for as long as he could remember, and the imperfections on his hands were a painful reminder that his efforts hadn't staved off the inevitability of aging. But there was nothing that could be done, and each morning invited a ritual acceptance of his circumstances. Death itself no longer frightened him, but a healthy mind and body was a terrible thing to lose.

As Abner sat up in bed, his daughter Caroline entered the room, wearing light blue scrubs. Her hair was different. She was always changing the color. He didn't understand why she felt the need to; he loved the natural black locks that she'd let drape over her shoulders. It reminded him of his mother. But Caroline had never met his mother. If he mentioned how lovely it was to be reminded of her, then maybe his daughter would keep it.

"Oh, Abner, don't get up. Hang on." Caroline rushed over, placing her small hands on his shoulders to help steady him as he shifted. "Good morning. Did you sleep well?"

"Fine, fine," he said. "I had a dream, but I can't seem to remember it. Funny how that happens, isn't it?"

Caroline reached into her front pocket and took out three orange pill bottles, placed two on the bedstand as she removed the top of one, and dropped a little white capsule into her palm. "It really is. Sometimes I wake up and all that's left is the feeling it gave me. But that's the best part, I think. Starts your day off right." She took the glass over to the sink, refilled it, and handed the glass with the pill to Abner.

He stared at the little capsule. "I don't need that, Caroline. And what happened to your hair? Why do that?" Abner took one of the blonde curls between his fingers and lifted it to her face. "I always thought it was wonderful the way it was."

Caroline softened her tone as if speaking to a child: "Abner, we've been through this. It will help. Don't you trust me?"

"Then, you take it. Silly girl," Abner scoffed. "I haven't taken medication all my life, and I'm as fit as I'll ever be."

"Please, Abner. For me."

He watched the light creases form at the corners of her mouth as she frowned. She looked so much younger lately. "Fine," he said. He took the pill from her hand, placed it on his tongue, and washed it away with a swig of water. "But when I start growing extra limbs, I know exactly who to blame when I call Social Services."

Caroline laughed, her face lighting up pink, showing the top row of teeth. "That seems only fair."

Abner paused, studying her face. "Have you had work done? I don't know how you can afford that on a painter's wages."

She ignored the question. "Would you like to listen to some music? And it's such a lovely day out, why don't we go for a walk around the garden while the sun's up? Then we can get you back for breakfast."

"I'm not hungry," said Abner. "Music, yes. Put something on. The records will gather dust and warp if they're not put to use."

Caroline walked to the cardboard box sitting beneath the windowsill. "Well, once we get some exercise, maybe afterward you will be. Your other pills need to be taken with food." She began rifling through its contents until pulling out a vinyl cover with the artwork peeling away at the corners.

"Other pills? Jesus, Caroline, are you trying to kill me?"

"No, Abner, I'm trying to help you. You're fussy this morning." She removed the record from its sleeve, fit it onto the player atop the windowsill, and placed the needle upon the black grooves. A soft and slow piano melody filled the room.

Abner closed his eyes, breathing in through his nose. "Wonderful choice. No one played the piano like Satie—except your mother. Do you remember her placing you on her lap while she played when you were little? It used to be the only thing that could stop you from crying. You were a loud, incessant child. It seems things never change." Abner opened one eye to wink and grin. "But don't think you're off the hook about this medication business. Do you even know what's in those things? You're an artist, not a nurse. For Christ's sake, I'd hardly trust your opinion on the matter."

Caroline pursed her lips and drifted over to the bedstand, eyeing the sheet of paper. "Did you read your letter?"

"What letter?"

"Your son left it for you." She tapped on the page and smiled, dimples forming on her cheeks with her teeth hidden.

"Adam? That bastard." Abner fumbled around in the drawer. "Good for nothing. He can write a damn letter but can't be bothered to visit his father? Caroline, where are my glasses?"

Caroline glanced around the room. "They're not in your drawer? That's where we always leave them."

"I know that. What the hell do you think I'm doing this for?" Abner began to tear through its contents, tossing photographs and empty pill bottles onto the floor. "See? They're not here." He slammed the drawer and shifted his feet flat on the ground. "I'll find them later. It can wait, I'm sure. Another pity plea asking to send more money for liquor—I know what he does with that damn money. Everything goes straight into his liver. If you can't trust a man with a drink, what else can't you trust him with?" Abner exhaled and pinched the bridge of his nose. "He could stand to be more like you, Caroline. You understand the duty of a daughter. Leaving an old man all alone like this, after all the years, all the money I threw into the trash for that boy—it's ingratitude. That's what it is."

One of the discarded photographs caught his eye. Abner leaned over with a grunt and picked up the Polaroid, bringing it close to his face as he squinted to focus upon the image it contained: Two young men sat together, their faces unblinking and blank, their leather jackets accentuated by the age and quality of the camera. He stared at the image for a long time, and Caroline leaned in to make sense of his reaction. "That's odd," he said. "How...odd."

Caroline said nothing but continued to watch Abner's facial muscles twitch and his brow furrow. Satie's piano weaved its way through the memory hidden in his mind somewhere behind the picture, filling the cracks that briefly glowed, but then floated away with the black and white moment into an empty chasm. "That's...odd," was again all he could muster about his recollection. "That looks almost like your brother, doesn't it? That looks like Adam."

Caroline placed her small hands upon his—the skin rough like worn leather but paper-thin—and gently coaxed the photograph out of his grasp. "Why don't we go for a walk? Maybe we'll find your glasses on the way."

His eyes followed the picture as it was placed back into the drawer. When it was gone, so too was the weak thread of something his brain had desperately clung to and almost held before slipping away. A profound sickness washed over Abner, and his hands began to tremble. A film of stinging tears welled from his eyes but stopped short of falling into the cracks carved throughout his face. There was a vague emptiness growing inside the ever-darkening recesses of his memories, where something important once existed, and without understanding what that something was, his mind remained just aware enough to grieve its absence. A flickering and dying light, swaying by a frayed cord attached to the ceiling of an empty room, still cast a weak shadow of the ghosts far deeper within.

Struck with unexplainable fear, Abner flailed before collapsing back onto the bed. His eyes searched the room, aching to find something within view that could provide an anchor to reality before the four walls fell away into a spiraling vacuum. "Something's not right," he sputtered. "Where am I?"

The nurse squatted before him to pull his erratic gaze back to her eyes. "Abner, breathe, honey. Breathe."

But Abner had found an anchor: Hung on the center wall by the locked door was an oil painting of the ocean, and a wide, sweeping, golden beach. He couldn't look away. The nurse's face blurred into his peripheries as the painted beach began to vibrate with life and memory.

She turned around to see what had magnetized Abner's attention, and unlocked the door, leaned out into the white hallway, and called out, "I need some help in here."

Abner shuffled across the room towards the painting that hummed in tune with his arrhythmic heartbeat. His fingers brushed against the acrylic colors, cold and distant to the touch, but something beneath them cried out behind his eyes. There was an ember somewhere in the void, and he could feel its warmth, but didn't know which direction would lead closer. Somewhere was a key that he had lost a long time ago when he had never realized there was anything to unlock.

Two orderlies rounded the hallway corner and entered the room with Abner's nurse. In one of their hands was a thin syringe. "It's happening again," said the nurse.

Abner paid no mind to the strangers who had joined. "My d—my daughter painted this." He pulled away from the painting to face her when he next spoke, his eyes glimmering and wide: "Caroline—my daughter painted this. Didn't she?"

"Yes," said the nurse. "It's lovely, isn't it? Why don't you just lie down, honey?"

"I don't understand." Abner held a trembling hand over his mouth, unable to keep his eyes away from the artwork. "I don't understand at all. Where— Where is my daughter? Where's Caroline? Someone, call her. Someone, call her NOW. I want to go home. I want to go home. I want to go home." The words swelled with anger, inflating until they burst, and released a torrent of fear before drowning beneath the sobs of a lost child. Abner wailed and cried, his legs giving out, and collapsed upon the floor. "Where is my daughter? Please help me. Someone, help me. Caroline."

The nurse sat down beside him, reached her arm around his wasting, convulsing frame, and whispered into his ear like a cooing mother, "*Shhh, honey, shhh. It's just a dream. You're just having a bad dream. It'll all be over soon.*" She nodded to the orderlies, and one of the men leaned on a knee with the syringe in hand, and, like a pinch from a ghost, the cocktail flooded into Abner's blood, and the world became very, very quiet.

There was a beach with golden sand, a young woman in a pink-striped bathing suit, and a boy and girl laughing in the shade beneath a leaning umbrella. Abner strained to put together their features, but the faces melted away into a gray blanket of static.

II.

You were born on New Year's Day, one minute past midnight in 1955. Your mother held you against her chest in a hospital bed somewhere in the United States, and she pointed out the window at the fireworks exploding in the sky and told you the world was celebrating your first breath.

Your father was a pilot in the Air Force, and he flew planes that dropped bombs on Korea. He drank and smoked and boxed and swore. You placed me on his withering body when I wasn't yet a year old, and he met his grandson for the first and last time as he lay dying in another hospital bed somewhere else in the United States. I don't remember this, but it's one of the things you still do, and you loved to tell me. He had two tattoos of gnomes on his chest. You still cry when you see one of the little statues in someone's garden. He must have been a lovely man.

When you were younger than me, you graduated college and joined the Peace Corps. You went to Morocco to teach children English. You learned to speak and write French and Arabic, and you smoked unfiltered cigarettes and hashish that you'd buy from the old men in the Marrakesh market. The local police once arrested you because you fit the profile of a white foreigner who had murdered a man in the town square. You were placed in a small and dirty jail cell, pressed against a wall by the other sweating bodies all packed into the space like sardines in a can. Twenty-four hours later, you were released, and you went to a café in the dry morning air to smoke cigarettes and drink ruby-red tea.

You would return from Morocco two years later, and promptly leave for Scotland and Ireland, spending time with extended family who lived in a little cottage in County Meath. They had acres of hilly green land and sheep, lots of sheep. Influenced by your Irish-Catholic roommates, you would become very religious for a time. You thought about becoming devout, dedicating yourself to the cloth and staying in your family's homeland. I don't know what caused you to change your mind, but I'm glad you did, because you came back to the United States and would meet your life partner, with whom you brought me into the world. It feels an odd thing to tell you, but I'm thankful that you did. Regardless of how many times I may have told you otherwise.

You were married twice. I don't know much about this first person. You never seemed to deem them worth mentioning. I know they were epileptic, and that you lived together in a trailer park outside of St. Louis. I don't know how you got there, or why you ended up there. I haven't asked you enough questions about your life. I'm sure you would have loved to tell me.

You met your life partner at an AA meeting. You weren't supposed to date others in recovery, but you did anyway, and, ten years later, you were married. You are over thirty years sober, and you still attend meetings when you can remember to. Because of you, I'm three months sober. You once showed me the little plastic baggie containing all of your chips, and, though you don't talk about it much, I could see the pride in your eyes for silencing a very loud demon. I am proud of you too. I hope you're proud of me.

The two of you found out you were pregnant with my sister on your wedding day. There were many things to celebrate that day. She's done the best she can, and she will be okay. I don't want you to worry about her. She looks like your mother. You loved to tell her that.

There's an old black-and-white photograph in your drawer of you sitting in the back of a car with your brother when you were nineteen. Your hair is long and wild and black, and your skin and your eyes are untouched by the passage of time. You showed me the picture when I was twenty, and it was like looking at a photo of myself in another life. I look so very much like you. One day I'll look like you do now, and I'll look back on my own photographs like you look upon that Polaroid in your dresser.

Your brother in the photo is now dead. You didn't attend the funeral. You didn't forget. You just refused to go. I don't mind telling you this because you didn't like your brother. I liked him fine, but I didn't know him like you did. There are many other siblings, and they live in different places. They love you, and they haven't forgotten. I don't want you to worry about them. We're all taken care of. You've done everything you needed to.

There are some things that I'm glad you won't recall, and they don't need to be remembered. Not everything is worth writing down or photographing or reminiscing on. Those things are lost in the ether, and you can rest knowing they won't return. I don't think on them either. Life is a long, long journey—even for me. Things change, and you are the most wonderful personification of that fact. That is all I wish for you to remember when it comes to these things. Dust blows away even when swept with the lightest breeze. The world moves forward. People do, too.

If there's anything else, I'll add it in here for you later. Take your medication and listen to Nurse Alice. She's the pretty blonde you like. She's a sweet person and is there to help you. Read this as many times as you need to. Don't worry about misplacing it. I can always write another one. I'll see you soon.

Your son,
Adam

Pink Elephants

If the spiders wouldn't bother him, Malcolm wouldn't bother them. They were large and black and hairy, and they moved across the pervasive shadows of the underlit, single-room apartment like computer glitches, transporting between different spots on the walls and ceiling without use of their legs.

He knew that what he was holding was a .22 caliber pistol, and that the clip held ten bullets with an eleventh in the chamber, which to his understanding was cocked and loaded. He knew the pistol was purchased illegally and that the serial number had been scratched off with a razor blade from a lime green box cutter. He had never fired a gun, let alone held one, and had been surprised to learn how heavy and solid such a small object could be as it trembled against the sweat coating his palm as his fingers curled around its grip.

He knew well enough from movies and pulp fiction novels that a .22 caliber bullet was unlikely to result in death unless aimed through the roof of the mouth at a forty-five-degree angle, providing the highest probability of severing the brain stem and cleanly exiting the base of the skull.

Malcolm had remained seated upon his bare soiled mattress, his back against the corner of the room to allow the widest berth from the spiders, staring at the pistol in his hand for the last three hours. This was because the precision and focus that the act required was impossible in his current state. The severity of his convulsions made a proper suicide something akin to performing open-heart surgery after ingesting a handle of vodka—an experience he'd welcome like the gates of Heaven, if only for the brief respite it would provide from his symptoms.

The spiders warped and elongated along the walls, never remaining the same size, undulating or pulsing like an erratic lifeline monitor. They'd left him well alone, but his mother standing in the opposite corner seemed to welcome their company, as many would appear and disappear up and down her body, covering the gaping and bleeding hole in the side of her head whilst they briefly found a home upon her face.

"You'll just fuck it up if you try," said his mother. "You've failed everything you've ever attempted. This won't be any different, Malcolm."

"Shut up," he said, studying the length of the barrel, refusing eye contact.

Grand mal seizures had come and gone about once every hour, he guessed, as the electronic alarm clock standing atop the cardboard box beside his mattress would read one time, and after blinking, read ten or fifteen minutes later as his blurred vision came back into focus, bringing with it a splitting headache and pains throughout his body that felt as if he'd just run a marathon in the moment spent outside consciousness.

"You'll miss and blow off your jaw," said his mother, the legs of a spider dangling over her bottom lip as it rested inside her slacked mouth. "No woman will ever love you. You'll have to wear a bag over your head when you go out in public. A disfigured freak hiding from the world."

"Shut up," said Malcolm.

"There wasn't a moment of hesitation for me. I had a plan and I executed it perfectly."

"I know," said Malcolm.

"You have too much of your father in you. You have coward's blood. I can't be blamed for your disappointment of a life. You would do well to remember that and thank your mother."

Malcolm didn't respond. The spiders were multiplying, eight-legged bodies erupting forth from one another like dividing cells across the ceiling.

"THANK YOUR MOTHER," she screamed. Black ooze dribbled down her chin as the spider disappeared from her mouth, as if it had been reduced to liquid underneath the force of her vitriol.

Malcolm picked up the alarm clock and hurled it at his mother, but it passed through her stomach like a stone into the fog and crashed against the wall.

"Ungrateful, little boy," she spat. "So ungrateful."

Malcolm reached into his pocket to pull out his phone, and typed **whr to cll if alchol withdraw** into the Google search bar, his hands shaking. Behind the cracks in the screen, he made out the first link with a number attached, and called, putting the phone on speaker, and placing it upon his lap.

A young woman's voice appeared, echoing against the walls: *"Wayward Wind Rehab and Detox Clinic, who am I speaking to?"*

"She can't help you," said his mother, the black liquid oozing down the side of her face from the open head wound.

"Malcolm," he said. "I'm Malcolm."

"Hi, Malcolm. What's going on?"

"I feel sick. I'm having withdrawals. I need to know if I should go to a hospital."

"They won't save you," said his mother.

"Okay. What are you withdrawing from, Malcolm?"

"Alcohol. I don't feel well."

"Okay. When was your last drink, Malcolm?"

"I don't remember. This isn't how I'm supposed to die. Do I need to go to a hospital?"

"She doesn't care about you," said his mother. "I care about you. Only your mother cares. But you won't listen to me. You never listened to me."

The sunlight behind the drawn shades of the sole window was disappearing behind the encroaching cloak of night. Shadows stretched across the ceiling and walls like an oil spill, and the spiders grew larger in size and number, strengthened by the darkness, coming closer, jumping in and out of reality as they approached.

"I can't answer that without seeing you," said the woman on the phone. *"We have availability for inpatient treatment in the next two weeks. Do you have medical insurance?"*

"Blood suckers," his mother hissed across the room. "Death merchants. Sickness profiteers. Vampires."

"I— That's not what I'm asking," Malcolm pleaded. "Just— can you help me? I don't know what to do right now."

"If you don't, is there someone who can help you pay out-of-pocket? It's a thousand dollars for a 28-day program. We can get you in, in two weeks. But if you have medical insurance—"

Malcolm hung up.

"I can help you, Son. Would you like Mommy to help you?"

Malcolm threw the phone at his mother, and, again, it passed through her forehead and shattered against the wall.

"Just like your father," she growled. "Always asking to clean up your messes, but never taking the help WHEN IT'S OFFERED. DO YOU WANT MOMMY TO HELP YOU, SON?"

Malcolm watched the spiders surrounding him, their red eyes and long, black fangs visible just over his head. Sucking away his soul with their vacant glares. He could feel the particles of his being leak out of him like a bloody nose, and float up as a fine gray mist absorbing into their hairy bodies, filling them up and engorging them—hundreds of spiders hanging upside-down directly above him, the size of human heads, blocking out any light until the room was pitch-black with a blanket of twitching, contorting creatures.

Through the stygian void, his mother stared. "Would you like this, sweetheart? Would you like Mommy to make it go away? To clean up your mess?" In her hand appeared a large bottle of vodka, glowing silver within the otherwise all-encompassing absence of light.

"No," he said.

Her face twisted into a scowl, her yellow teeth bared like a rabid dog. "No? NO? YOU UNGRATEFUL LITTLE BOY." His mother launched across the room, her feet stamping upon the floor like exploding mortars.

Thousands of little red eyes pierced through him like radioactive fallout from every corner of the room, the walls alive with spiders, squirming and shifting like one massive organism, collapsing in on him as she shrieked.

"YOU WILL NEVER LEARN UNLESS I TEACH YOU. BUT YOU NEVER. FUCKING. LISTEN." His mother's face was an inch away from his, the putrid stench of death leaking out from the rotting hole in her head, from the black ooze dripping from her teeth and leaking from her eyes.

The only time he had ever seen his mother cry.

"I'LL DO IT MYSELF. LIKE I ALWAYS DID."

She grasped on to the pistol in his hand, spiders crawling down her arm like real animals, leaping onto his chest and neck, the bristling hairs on their legs like hypodermic needles sinking into his flesh.

The walls melted as the massive wave of creatures converged upon him from every direction.

"HELP MOMMY HELP YOU."

Through the blinding pain, the world around him sinking into a pool of black ooze and constricting, hairy limbs, Malcolm squeezed shut his eyes and pulled back the hammer.

"SHUT. UP."

The barrel plunged into his mother's mouth and erupted with a brilliant white light. The clip unloaded into the back of her skull until he heard a *click*.

All at once, the weight of a thousand creatures lifted off his body. A sliver of yellow moonlight seeped into the room, glowing through his eyelids.

Malcolm opened his eyes.

His mother stood before him, the miasma of pus and rotting meat evaporating behind the smell of gunpowder. A trickle of gray smoke floated up to the bare ceiling from the hole in her head. "Didn't think you had it in you," she said, then dissolved before him like dust blown away in the wind.

Malcolm sat up, upon the soiled mattress in the corner of his one-room apartment, alone.

Begotten

Growing out of adolescence was like emerging from a dense fog. You breathe better, the things around you become easier to identify. You retain the shape of things in your mind, their smell and significance. They don't run through your fingers after leaving your sight but adhere to the walls of your skull like nicotine stains. You don't know their significance until after the fact because you're able to replay the imagery by picking off the residue left behind. Everything leaves a trail inside you. Every experience becomes part of you. It's new and exciting and terrifying to be so intertwined with the world outside your mind.

What happened was like a traumatic brain injury, they said. It damages you. It leaves you unable to retain the moments before and after as well. They're deemed collateral byproduct of being within proximity to the event. The moment that is submerged by the brain becomes a sinkhole that changes the landscape of everything absorbed nearby. Years are lost, compartmentalized into solitary, abstract shards that are forced to encapsulate the entire developmental period. Childhood becomes a fractured bone that was never set, so healed improperly. Which is to say, it never healed at all.

The brain is malleable. The brain rewires itself. The brain finds a way to ensure survival. What disappears is what must disappear. These are necessary martyrs to keep the event at the bottom of the sinkhole. The brain knows most of all that it must survive. The threat to that survival must stay submerged, as deep as possible. It doesn't matter what else drowns with it, as long as the event can't resurface for air.

From that moment forward, the brain's mission is to encourage anything that will keep the event from getting oxygen. Collateral damage is inevitable.

Everything must go.

I looked again at the piece of torn paper. It was the right house, I accepted that.

I had no preconception as to its appearance, but still what I saw felt wrong and alien. It was a modest home painted an unattractive white that had turned yellow with age, gnarled like the pages of a book left out in the rain. The lawn was manicured and watered, maintained to a degree that didn't match the neighborhood. It was late afternoon and the streetlights had yet to turn on, the setting sun dousing the street with an amber glow. There were no children out playing, but, through the windows, I could see televisions blaring.

The curtains on his house were drawn. Through his windows, I could see nothing.

I stepped onto the porch and the old wood sighed and creaked beneath my feet. My mind was muddled, and all I could tell it was that there was still time. There was time to leave or to wait, and, after that, it said nothing. My lungs convulsed, and air was hard to find, and my legs had no strength to give, so I sat down on the rocking chair as if it were my own. There was still time, it said to me. And I agreed. There's still time, I replied.

I reached into my coat pocket, removed the clear plastic bottle, disregarding the cold and solid object nestled beside it, and drank more while watching the sunset as the amber turned to gold-lined silhouettes. My lungs inflated with air, and my legs found strength, and I rocked back and forth for a while, understanding that quiet was the eye of the storm. There's still time, I said. There's still all the time in the world.

From the moment I discovered its efficacy, drinking alcohol became a balancing act. You drink enough and the swords in your chest dislodge, the fear melts into the floor, and you are content. Euphoric, even—a sensation so foreign that you understand why the Mesopotamians saw beer as a gift from the gods. Nothing works like alcohol; no mixture of pills, sex, violence, or apathy comes close to the respite provided by that magical potion. But as you continue to drink—and you always will—you inevitably lose your balance and fall into the very same pit that the drink had levitated you out from. Though, in your absence, shovels had been taken to the earth, and the pit you now exist within is miles deeper. It's at this point that the images you poisoned your liver to banish return to the forefront of your mind like ayahuasca visions. The sinkhole your subconscious so diligently created begins to vomit up the imprisoned event in fragments. They are the Titans breaking free from the depths of Tartarus. They rearrange before your eyes to become the silenced memory and it plays in flashes, something unknown to you but painfully familiar. It's like self-inflicted déjà vu, a wormhole carved into the fabric of the universe to bring you an alternate reality that cannot be yours, but is.

That's when I see his face. I see it in great detail. I know who he is, and I know what he's doing, his movements, and it can't be true—my brain tells me it isn't. But it can no longer be trusted. I've torn down the heavy walls, and the brain lacks its defenses. It's like staring into the sun. The pain is too real for what created it not to be. The atmosphere has been destroyed, and the radiation becomes me.

In the morning, I will forget.

I placed the empty bottle on the porch, stood up, and knocked on the door.

An older woman answered, only a sliver of her face visible through the chain-locked crack. "We don't want it," she said. But she didn't close the door. A single blue-gray eye stared at me.

"I'm not selling anything, ma'am." I let the alcohol pull a friendly smile across my face. "I was looking for Ray. Is he home?"

"Raymond? He's not expecting any visitors. What do you want?"

I answered reflexively: "Counsel. We used to know each other, he and I."

The woman scanned me up and down, the blue-gray eye shimmering as it stopped to focus on my face. "You're not even half his age. He's not practicing anymore. Raymond's retired."

"Is he?" I said, feigning sincerity. "He always had time to help when I was younger. I've come a long way, ma'am. Would it hurt to let me in at least? A glass of water maybe?"

She continued staring through the crack in the door, but her face relaxed. It showed her age: her wrinkles, her liver spots.

When it became clear she wasn't going to respond, I pushed again: "I don't mean to be a nuisance. I just came a long way, is all. He may remember me."

The door closed. I heard the fumbling of metal. The woman reappeared, the doorway open. She was short and plump, in a hand-stitched sweater. Her hair matched her eyes, stopping short of her chin. "What did you say your name was?"

"I didn't. It's Martin—Marty. He may remember me as Marty."

"From where?" she asked, but I had already walked inside.

The living room smelled of heavy cleaner and mothballs. Like an assisted care facility. The air was thick with the smell of the elderly. Atop the fireplace was a large, wooden crucifix. There were no photos, no animals, nothing personal on display. It felt empty. I was glad there were no pets. It would be much harder if there were pets.

The woman retreated to the kitchen, poured a glass of water, and handed it to me. "He's just resting," she said. "Let me go check on him and see if he can talk. He's not in the best of health these days."

I nodded and waited for the woman to disappear down a hallway. She opened a door and slid inside before softly closing it behind her. The glass in my hand had little flowers painted on the outside, their details chipping off from years of use and cleanings. The water tasted like copper.

A group of orange pill bottles sat on the kitchen counter. I began picking them up, looking for words I recognized: hydroxyurea, methotrexate, Afinitor, cyclophosphamide, hydroxydaunorubicin, Oncovin, prednisone. These were meaningless to me, of no use. But also in the cache were three I did know: OxyContin, Demerol, and hydrocodone. Beautiful, colorful little pills.

I leaned out into the hallway and heard low murmurs between two people coming from inside the room. The man's voice was slurred and irritable.

Six Oxys, one Demerol, and three hydrocodone slid down my throat with a gulp of water. I would have liked to crush and snort them but was glad I hadn't when the woman returned as soon as I put the bottles back in their place.

"He's tired," she started. "But he doesn't get many visitors, so he'd like to see you. Raymond says he's sorry he doesn't remember you. You can follow me, but you need to keep it short. He's in and out these days. Be patient with him."

The woman urged me towards the hall and directed me inside. The stench of putrefaction struck the moment I stepped through the doorway. It was a unique scent, one I'd only encountered once before.

I'd been working at a restaurant years earlier when a large family came in to sit down. One of them was very old. Immediately, a noxious miasma began floating in the air, attaching to every molecule of the room. Each time I had to go over to that section, the smell was overpowering. Some customers asked their servers if they could be moved to a different table. We all smelled it, we all tried not to breathe, as if a chemical weapon had been released, but no one spoke of it.

When the family left, one new hire began bussing the table. I didn't want to join her, but it was clear that none of the other staff were going to submit to the stink that wafted over the room like an aimless, exorcised demon. When I reluctantly came to help, she talked about the thing no one else would. Happily, she talked about it. I always remembered that, how odd it was. She seemed chipper to get the opportunity to explain to someone what she knew.

This server had worked for many years at a cancer ward. She had experienced that exact, specific stench many times. "That old man is dying," she told me. "He's at the very end of his life. That's when they begin to smell like that. It's the smell of their body rotting on the inside. It's the effluvia emitted during the process of death. There were other people who probably recognized it too," she told me, "but people don't like to acknowledge that kind of reality. The reality of what comes with an expiring body, an expiring human life." She said this all with a smile, cleaning off the bits of food that had dribbled onto the table from the old man's quivering lips, piling up the dishes before walking away. That smell stayed wafting across the restaurant for a full two days after the old man left. As if he left us with a piece of his extinguishing soul. Wherever he went, dropping breadcrumbs leading back to what would inevitably be a bloated corpse.

I didn't need to understand what the names of those pills meant. The stench in Raymond's room told me everything.

He sat in the corner, a blanket covering his legs. His face was gaunt and flushed red, the salt-and-pepper goatee still there. A flash of hidden memory erupted before my eyes, superimposed over the real man. Movements—the lurching, back and forth. Soft eyes. Focused eyes. Unfeeling in every facial feature but the eyes. Even their color escaped me inside the memory. He was already an older man when I knew him, and the progression had done him no favors.

It's difficult to get a read on the true size of a man when you're just a child. The whole world was large and frightening. He felt like a large man then, his robes adding layers of weight to his frame. He was a presence that inspired comfort—until he didn't. A bear of a man. But sitting across the room, he was frail, skeletal. I didn't know if I was supposed to feel dread, or confliction, but I felt nothing. Not even anger. He was the empty hole, a blip of static in a stream of uneven recollection. He was the ghost of a cavity.

I sat down at the desk across from Raymond. It had been thoroughly cleaned and the smell that mixed with what came from within the old man made me dizzy. There was a single tome atop the desk next to a pair of readers, and it was opened to a bookmarked page: ***The Book of Acts. Verse 2:38*** was unevenly underlined with black marker. The words blended and shifted on top of one another. I blinked hard and directed my eyes back towards Raymond. "Hi, Ray," I said.

He looked at me for a long time before answering, his eyes pockets within black circles. The only evidence that he was still alive was the rattling, hoarse whine that escaped his lips each time he exhaled.

The woman watched us both from the open doorway.

"Hello," he said. "I've met you. Have I met you?"

There were no photographs on the walls. A single bookshelf stood beside the old man, filled with hardcovers that smelled like sour pine.

"Yes," I said. "A long time ago. If you don't remember me, that's okay."

He wore a heavy knitted sweater. With the blanket beneath, it looked like a straitjacket pinned to his body. "No one calls me that anymore."

"Ray?" I answered. "That's how I knew you then. Would you like me to call you Raymond?"

"Doesn't matter." Bitterness masked by distant nostalgia coated his words like poison on an arrow.

"You don't wear the collar anymore. Do you still have it? Did they let you keep it?"

"They don't let you keep anything. They took everything."

"That must have been difficult."

"Doesn't matter," he said again. "What do you want?"

The woman caught the spite injected into his response and cut in: "Raymond isn't used to visitors, don't take it to—"

"You don't need to talk for me," he interrupted. "I can talk how I want. So, what do you want?"

"I just wanted to ask some questions. I'd like some guidance, Father. Do I still call you Father?"

Raymond's face froze and the rattling ceased before whatever that word had brought into his mind vanished. "Doesn't matter," he said. "What's your name again? How do you know me? I don't know you."

I wished the woman would just leave. She was making this harder. Words were becoming slippery, harder to grasp before forming on my tongue. I took too many. You're not supposed to take that many. I couldn't remember how much I drank. I couldn't remember much at all. The light was getting dim. There was no easy way around this.

"I went to school at St. Anthony's. Do you remember St. Anthony's, Father? ...Ray?"

His face erupted with emotion, and, for a moment, I saw what existed in the pockets of my subconscious. The entirety of his flickering lifeforce stoked a fire of terror inside his eyes.

I thought that would make me feel good. I felt nothing.

The woman moved from the doorway to stand between Raymond and me. "You need to leave. Now. My brother's done his time. He's done his penance. There's double jeopardy—I looked it up—so there's nothing more you can do now. You wanna sue? He doesn't have a thing left to his name. He's an old man, what more do you all want from him? Shame on you. Get out." The woman stood tall and rigid, pointing towards the exit like a schoolmarm directing me to detention. Like it was going to make a difference.

I pulled out the pistol from my coat pocket and rested it on my lap. "Listen,"—I vigorously shook my head, trying to dissolve the fog between my ears, and used the barrel of the gun to scratch my temple—"I just have some questions, ma'am. I'm gonna ask them, and then I'm gonna be on my way. Why don't you sit down?"

She reached into her pocket—a really bold thing to do—and I pointed the weapon at her chest.

"I need you to drop that. Right on the floor, ma'am. Please."

The cell phone slid from her hand, and she held her palms out. "Don't hurt me."

"I'm not here to hurt anybody. I just wanna talk." Keeping the pistol trained on the woman, I looked back towards Raymond, who hadn't moved or reacted at all. "I just wanna ask some questions."

There were two of the old man in front of me now, but a single voice came out: "You go ahead and shoot me."

"No, no, look—no." I lowered the gun. "I don't know what you did. To those kids. I don't hate you. I don't feel much of anything. But there's been...this shadow hanging over me my whole life. I just need to know if it's you."

Raymond sat up as much as he could—as if he were feeding off what little power that he had over me. "I don't know what you're talking about."

"Sure," I said. "Sure." Something was draining from my body, not what was fed to Raymond, but something more substantial. I could feel it pooling at my feet, taking with it any warmth and strength that remained. I'd taken too many. I made a mistake. I'd taken too many. "I remember some of it. I remember the parish house across the street from the church. I remember the basement. I remember you, Father Ray." Beads of sweat formed at my hairline. My hands were clammy. Sick, I felt sick.

"You read what everyone else read in the newspaper. You can't fool me. You're not the first to come here with lies...slander. Hungry for attention."

I pressed the barrel of the pistol against his cheek. My legs felt like splintering sticks. "I've done...bad things, Father. I've done awful things in my life. I am not here to force out your guilt. Please, just tell me what happened. It's this...hole in me, this black hole. It's sucked up everything good in the world, pulled it all from out my hands—and I can't even see what's inside it. All I know, at the very bottom..."—I pulled back the hammer and pushed the metal deeper into his rubbery flesh—"is your face. And you can lie and lie and lie until a bullet finds your skull, or that cancer rots through your organs, but I won't live like that. I know what's in that book over there. You all burned it into me for years, the words on that page. So don't you pretend that you don't know. Don't do that to me. Absolve me, Father. I can't be bothered with your guilt. Your anguish. Tell me you caused this. Tell me you ruined me, so I can know, and I can pull this weight off my chest. You owe me that much."

The woman snapped, her whole body trembling, her face red as a sunrise: "For God's sake, Raymond, tell him the truth! Give him what he wants before he kills us!"

Maybe an answer was going to come. If I had a moment longer.

My heart skipped a beat. It skipped a beat, and I waited for the next, but it never came. My lungs refused air. I heard myself choke. As if I were standing beside myself, I heard it. The face in the sinkhole, the face before me, darkened, and the room narrowed, and the white ceiling became my view, and I heard the *thump* of a body hitting the carpeted floor, and the gun on the carpet beside it, and I saw the old man, the face in the sinkhole, pick up the gun without a word or hesitation, and press it against his temple, and I saw the flash, and I heard the woman scream, and I saw the blood and brain matter spray the ceiling, and the world went quiet and black.

A life flashed before me. A short and uneven road, unpaved but well-traveled. It wasn't until just after, in those timeless milliseconds, I passed the abyss of memory, that I realized how many were still left to cross. How many I had dug myself. What a difficult road it was that I'd created. It would have taken another lifetime to fill them all.

I hope he goes to Heaven.

Then I'll know there's a place for me, too.

An Occurrence At The Funeral Of Joshua Miller

It was a beautiful day at the cemetery.

Michael had wished for rain so the family would be forced to dirty their rented formalwear, standing in an inch of mud, leaving stains that could never be cleaned. Each time they would return to the grave for the rest of their lives, they would be reminded of those soiled clothes like the soiled, rotting heart of their precious deceased. But, being a clear morning, Michael could have a view, unobstructed by rainfall, of their faces twisted up in pain, bloated and red from tears. He would see directly into their shrink-wrapped eyes and drink in the agony, knowing that a piece of that feeling would remain buried inside them like a virus until they joined their flesh-and-blood's corpse beneath the earth.

He took solace in that.

Michael stepped out of his car in the parking lot, his scuffed and torn tuxedo serving as attire for the funeral he wasn't invited to and as celebratory garments the night before. Crushed beer cans fell from the passenger seat onto the concrete. He reached into his interior jacket pocket, removed the fifth of whiskey and took a long pull as his bleary eyes adjusted to the sunlight.

Letting the bottle dangle at his side, Michael stumbled across the lawn dotted with gravestones, towards the small circle of mourners gathered around a coffin.

"Tell me again. Read it again! Slower this time."

Anthony eyed him warily as Michael laughed and threw his head back to drink the shot. He picked up the pamphlet from the bar and read: *"Please join us to celebrate the life of JOSHUA*

MILLER, beloved son and brother, December 16th, 2018. We will be gathering to share our fondest memories of Joshua. We please ask that this be a celebration for friends and family only." Anthony repeated the final line as a grin stretched across Michael's face: "For friends and family only."

"Can I have that?" Michael reached over the pint glasses between them and snatched the pamphlet before his friend could answer. He took a pen resting atop a settled bar tab and began scribbling on the paper.

Anthony nipped at his beer. "Why do you want it?"

Without taking his eyes off his task, Michael responded, "I'm gonna put it up on my wall. Maybe get it framed. There—I fixed it." He lifted the pamphlet to show Anthony, still grinning. The black-and-white photograph of Joshua Miller had been adorned with a crudely drawn penis ejaculating onto the dead man's face, with devil horns and an X over each blank eye. "This may be some of my best work." Michael stared at Anthony, hoping for a reaction and, upon getting nothing in response, he slammed his open hand on the bar and cackled before draining the remainder of his beer glass in a single, gluttonous swig. "Lighten up, man." He belched, wiped the foam from his neglected facial hair, and held up two fingers towards the bartender. "This is the best day of my fucking life. Can you try to be happy for me?"

Anthony ignored the fresh shot glasses placed in front of them. "I don't know how to talk to you right now. Whatever..."—he waved his hands in circles around Michael—"this is...it's not healthy. You should talk to somebody about this. I wanna help, but—"

"Help?" Michael interrupted. "Help? What're you talking about? I'm fine! I'm better than fine! I'm the happiest I've fucking been since that..."—he paused, searching for a word that would inject the heaviest dose of venom—"faggot did, what he fucking did to me." He picked up one of the shots, clacked it against the other still sitting on the bar, and held the glass in front of his chin. "To the death of Joshua Miller. Ding-dong, the witch is fucking dead! Haha!" The cheap whiskey disappeared down his throat as he shivered and grimaced.

Anthony watched the mechanical motion, contemplating how best to breach the topic he wished to address. He lifted the glass, staring at the brown liquor before throwing it into the back of his throat. "Just tell me you're not gonna do what you're thinking of doing."

Michael's eyebrows raised as he smirked, accentuating the lines like trenches running across his forehead. "Now, what would YOU possibly think that I'M thinking of doing?"

"Just don't go, man. Don't show up there."

"I'm not gonna do that. I wouldn't do that. Why would I do that?" Michael's eyes widened and bore into Anthony's. They burned and glimmered underneath the dim bar lights. Lifting two fingers again in the air, he spoke softly, almost unintelligibly, beneath the blaring music pouring out across the room: "I'll tell you what I'm gonna do. I'm gonna piss on his fucking grave. I'll destroy his tombstone. And every time they fix it, I'll come back and destroy it again. And every night, I'll pray there's an afterlife, because I want him looking up from the fucking Hellfire, watching me do it—over and over." His voice rose, the hatred spilling out over his swollen tongue. "Over and fucking over, I'll do it. Until I know that, somewhere, he's screaming at me to stop."

Anthony grabbed the new round of shots as they arrived, pulling them out of Michael's reach. "Let's call it a night, buddy. Sleep this off."

Michael slumped forward, rubbing his palms over his face. "Fine, you go. Just leave." The words slithered out between gritted teeth. "I paid for those, leave them there. You go."

Anthony looked around the bar. "I don't know if I can leave you here alone. Why don't we get outta here?"

"I'm not alone." Michael grasped Anthony's hand to lift it away from the glasses and took both, sliding them in front of his stooping body. "I'll be fine. I'll be fine. Let me just sit here a while."

Michael drank both shots before gagging and turning around in his barstool to solidify the end of their interaction. As Anthony stood to leave, placing a hand on his shoulder, Michael mumbled something into his empty glass.

"What was that?" asked Anthony.

Michael glanced back for a moment before facing the bartender with a finger in the air. "Nothing. I'll see you later." He waited for the feeling of eyes on his back to dissipate, picked up the drink, and repeated it for only himself to hear: "I wish I had killed him."

The courage bubbling within Michael's chest transmuted into acute terror as the eyes of those in attendance turned to identify the drunken stranger charging across the grass. Even as a body in the dirt, Joshua Miller held a chokehold over his emotions. His specter had climbed atop Michael's shoulders, weakening his legs like iron shackles strapped to his ankles. He had never met the people who all now stared at him, but, in their features, he saw Joshua's face. The mother and father, bearing his eyes and thin nose, and the brother, a young child with tousled brown hair who was unaware of the black mold that encompassed his soul by birthright. The instinct to rip out their tongues and eyes was immediately traded for the horror of recognition for what they represented.

Before Michael could relinquish the scream rising to the lump in his throat, the priest at the head of the congregation interrupted his own speech and waved. "Hello," he said.

Michael fell to a knee and vomited. Every repressed memory played inside his head thousands of times like a short film, then poured out onto the earth, twisted up in the rejected liquor and the blood like wet coffee grounds from stomach ulcers.

A collective gasp emitted from the onlookers. A woman—the mother—stumbled forward and bent down close to his face.

Michael wiped away the bile and met her gaze. Behind the mascara running down her cheeks like water droplets on a dirty mirror, he recognized the same eyes he'd seen in his nightmares for seven years. "GET AWAY." The words erupted from somewhere hidden deep inside him, in a voice he didn't recognize and couldn't control. "STAY AWAY FROM ME." Michael fell backwards, reaching his arms behind him to crawl away like an injured animal. He pulled out the whiskey bottle and began swinging it like a blunt weapon. Terror wrapped itself around his throat and strangled his next words, expelling from his mouth as guttural moans.

As the rest of the audience stood watching in silence, the father stepped forward, around the coffin suspended above its grave, and pulled his wife away from the man sputtering on the ground. "He needs help! Call 9-1-1!"

"NO!" Michael screamed, the acrid taste of stomach acid coating the inside of his mouth. He lifted himself back onto his knees, wobbling as he found the strength to stand. "Let me talk!" Michael aimed a rigid finger like a sniper's laser at the coffin before them. "It's...ALL...*his fault.*"

Michael had the better part of a decade to think of ways to torture Joshua Miller. For the first three or so years after the event, he could do nothing but drink in bed and sleep away the hours with a box cutter underneath his pillow. But, as time went on, he formulated plans to ambush Joshua Miller with a baseball bat or a dull knife—something that would take time to kill someone. He would start by breaking the kneecaps or severing tendons in the ankles, and then, as Joshua Miller lay there gasping, unable to run, his eyes screaming upon recognizing his assailant, Michael would slice open his throat. Not deep enough for him to bleed out, but, if done with surgical precision, Michael could reach inside the wound and tear out his vocal cords. He'd then use a lighter and a sewing needle to cauterize the gash so Joshua Miller couldn't speak as he continued.

Michael understood he lacked the constitution to enact this plan but surmised that, with enough bloodlust and alcohol to cloud his terror response and judgment, it could be pulled off. Disposing of the body or covering up the murder would be unnecessary, as Michael planned to kill himself upon completion. Suicide by cop was a possibility, as he could call in his own crime and wait atop the corpse, soaked in blood, speaking his last words to the emergency operator to be recorded and immortalized for the family and world to know exactly why Joshua Miller was killed. Michael was not a violent man beyond this hypothetical circumstance, and wouldn't hurt the police, but he would scare them and, for that, they would kill him.

Joshua Miller was also not an innocent man long before doing what he did to Michael. It was feasible to tip the police on any number of the illegal activities he knew Joshua Miller regularly participated in. The justice system could then ruin his life. If this were to happen, he had dreams of becoming famous— for what was of no consequence, as the sole reason for achieving notoriety was to have a podium with a large audience. Perhaps after being invited on a talk show, Michael could swim through the monotony of questions and answers, ask for a moment to speak, face the camera, and announce that there was an inmate named Joshua Miller in So and So Penitentiary.

Michael would then address the inmates at that particular penitentiary and tell them that whoever is willing to beat and sodomize Joshua Miller on a regular basis for the remainder of his sentence, he would then donate a large sum of his fortune to their commissary fund. Upon receiving an agreement to the proposal, Michael would then give that inmate the entirety of his assets, and kill himself.

However these fantasies played out, the constant was that at their conclusion Michael would no longer be alive. There was nothing left about life that held any purpose other than enacting revenge on Joshua Miller. Everything else had been taken away. After that, he could rest.

But Joshua Miller was dead—through circumstances outside of Michael's control. He died not caring or knowing about the effects of his actions, not understanding the depths of the black chasm to which he had sent his victim, not expending an ounce of remorse for the life he'd destroyed in the wake of his violent, otherwise unremarkable existence. Joshua Miller was dead, and the gaping hole he'd left in Michael's psyche would continue to bleed out and decay, for, not only was he the one who had administered the poison, but he was the single person in the world who, unwittingly or not, held its antidote. And with the stillness of Joshua Miller's once beating heart, that antidote forever disappeared from the face of the earth.

With adrenaline cascading throughout his body, the cloud of anxiety was disappearing behind his rage. Michael approached the coffin, the mourners all backing away as he wound up and kicked the solid mahogany, resulting in a dull *thud* and pain like an electric shock running up his leg. "FUCK YOU," he screamed, kicking the coffin over and over, letting the agony tear through the bones in his feet.

"FUCK YOU." *Thud.* "FUCK YOU." *Thud.* "FUCK YOU." *Thud.*

The father charged forward and strangled Michael from behind with an arm around his neck, pulling him away from his deceased son. Michael swung the whiskey bottle over his shoulder, smashing it into the father's nose, which erupted a stream of blood like a broken spigot. The father went limp and collapsed onto the ground.

People screamed and scattered as some pulled out their phones to call the police. The child fell to his knees beside his father, bawling in an earsplitting pitch like a teakettle.

"IT ISN'T FAIR," Michael roared, hurling his fist at the coffin, shattering his free hand. "YOU DON'T GET TO JUST DIE. YOU DESERVED TO FUCKING SUFFER. YOU CAN'T JUST GET AWAY WITH IT."

The mother let out a bloodcurdling howl, like a dog caught in a trap.

This brought Michael's surroundings back into focus, and he turned to face the screaming woman, his nostrils flared and eyes alight, his mind on fire. "SHUT THE FUCK UP. SHUT UP. YOU DID THIS." He turned again to point at the bleeding man on the ground. "YOU RAISED A FUCKING MONSTER. DO YOU KNOW WHAT HE'S DONE? DO YOU?"

The father spit up crimson and mumbled something incoherent. The priest took off down the lawn, waving down people and yelling as they walked past. God had left this place.

Michael opened the bottle still in his hand, now smeared with blood, and drank until coughing up liquor as it ran down into his windpipe. "YOUR SON RUINED...EVERYTHING." He threw his arms out in exasperation, sloshing whiskey onto the dirt as if blessing the site with tainted holy water. Michael leaned down close to the father, lowering his voice to a hiss: "*What did you do to make him the way he was?*"

Sirens began crying in the distance.

Punctuated by whimpers, the mother's voice called to him: "Please...don't hurt him anymore. Please don't. What do you *want* from us?"

Michael spun around, watching the woman inching over to reach an arm around her son and pull him close. The family of Joshua Miller sat crouched beside his splintered coffin, gazing up at a man they'd never before seen.

He looked out over the graveyard, at the brightness of the winter morning burning his eyes, at the faint glow of approaching red and blue lights through the treeline. "I want you—I want you to make this go away." Michael's nervous system collapsed in on itself. Tears welled and his words broke into sobs that trembled inside his stomach like the wails of purgatorial spirits. He thrust the side of his fractured hand into the center of his chest. "Just make this go away. I can't handle it anymore. I can't."

"I don't know what to say to you," the mother cried. "I don't know who you are! I don't know what he did to you. I don't know, I don't know, I don't know, I don't *understand!* My son is dead! I don't know *WHO YOU ARE!*"

Three police cars pulled into the parking lot. The figurine men drew their pistols and grew larger as they sprinted across the grass.

Michael spoke, his eyes trained on the approaching police he decided would end his life: "Tell me you're sorry."

The woman stared at him, mouth agape. "I—I don't—"

"GOD DAMNIT!" Michael dug his nails into his scalp, tearing at the hair until he could feel it rip and his vision went white. He hurled the bottle at the ground, the shattered glass like bomb shrapnel, twinkling in the sunlight around the family. "SAY YOU'RE FUCKING SORRY. TAKE IT AWAY FROM ME."

"OKAY," the mother shouted, her eyes darting towards the police feet away from their target, "I'M SORRY. OKAY? I'M SORRY YOU'RE SO SICK."

"THAT'S NOT—"

Michael's response was severed as a policeman collided into his chest with the full force of his body.

He hit the earth.

The men rolled him onto his stomach and attached handcuffs to his wrists as a boot found the side of his head.

"I'M SORRY YOU'RE SICK," the mother repeated, cowering from the crazed man being lifted to his feet.

"SAY IT AGAIN."

A punch landed against his ribs, blood streaming down his face, the grass flattening beneath him, leaving a trench in the earth as they dragged him away from the convulsing woman.

"I'm *SORRY!*" she called to him.

"SAY IT AGAIN!"

"*I'M SORRY.*"

He saw the mother shrink away between the gravestones, and, still, he screamed: "*AGAIN.*"

A large hand grasped the back of his neck and squeezed, twisting it around to face him towards the open door of the cruiser. He looked up to the blinding sky. "AGAIN. SAY IT AGAIN. SAY IT AGAIN."

No response came but the muffling of the outside world. The door slammed shut. He bashed his head into the separating bars. "AGAIN. AGAIN. AGAIN. AGAIN. AGAIN."

Thud. Thud. Thud. Thud. Thud.

The cold midnight air raised the hairs on Michael's bare leg as he stepped onto the lawn. He reached down to unfurl the cuff in his jeans, covering up the ankle monitor. Carefully, he crept around the flat marble gravestones, illuminated by the sparse light of the crescent moon behind the clouds, and approached the etched stone standing upright beyond a patch of new grass. He sat upon the earth cross-legged, pulled off the gym bag strapped around his shoulder, and leaned in close to read the words:

Joshua Miller
1994 – 2018
God needed another angel in Heaven.

Michael laughed. He reached into the bag, removed a pint of Old Crow whiskey, twisted off the plastic top, and drank. It had rained earlier in the night, so the wet grass soaked the bottom of his jeans.

A cemetery was a tranquil place during the night. It was quiet, and he imagined the spirits of the dead rose with the moon to sit beside him and listen to the wind. Michael imagined Joshua Miller was watching him.

He smiled and smiled and continued to drink until the bodily urge came. Michael stood, undid the button on his pants, and pulled out his cock. The dark yellow stream of urine polished the stone as it ran down its face, absorbing into the dirt at its foundation. He stepped away, tucked himself inside his pants, reached back into the gym bag and pulled out the ten-pound sledgehammer, letting it rest over his shoulder.

Michael craned his neck, looking up at the night sky, and suckled at the pint until the last of the cheap whiskey tore through his throat and settled like burning gasoline at the base of his stomach. He dropped the empty bottle beside the gravestone, grasped the sledgehammer with both hands, lifted it high over his head, and swung at the glistening marble slab like a crusader dealing a deathblow with a claymore.

A large chunk broke off with a metallic *bang*, echoing across the flat landscape. Michael giggled and looked around before swinging again, knocking off another piece, tearing Joshua away from his surname. Again, the sledgehammer collided, again, again, again, again until what stood before him were the crumbled remains of Joshua Miller's memory.

Breathing heavily, Michael released the weapon and leaned over with his hands on his knees, laughing. He laughed until the sound carried over the treeline, until its volume surpassed the act that had brought it on.

Once he ejected the last of the joy from within his chest like air in a vacuum, Michael allowed silence to return. He collapsed upon the earth, straightened himself, and returned to a meditative, cross-legged posture. The silence encompassed him, seeping into the cracks left unmended, until it suffocated the fire he'd kept stoked since the first day of his second life. His mind became empty and hollow. The cold he'd staved off for so long soaked into his aching bones, and he accepted the flood of emotions he'd buried like a stillborn child. They came in waves, rising up and up and up until his nose submerged under their weight, and he could no longer breathe.

Michael remained there, floating in the murky depths, refusing to fight its violent current as the pressure of his environment crushed his body, the corpse of a specter beneath his feet far below, and he peered through the blackness at the rubble he'd created.

The fractured pieces glinted with the silver moonlight, the words etched upon them now illegible.

He had made his statement.

Michael would remain in the graveyard, waiting, engulfed. He would wait until he heard an answer.

And when it came, when the voice cried out from a place it could never leave, he would reject it. He would stand up, with air in his lungs, and he would walk away.

He would wait as long as it took.

The Last Cowboy

The fuck you expect me ta say?

Sorry? You want me ta cry? Plead? Scream? You want me ta look y'all in the eyes, red-faced and remorseful? Well, fuck you.

No, I'm not done.

I see your hand itchin', sir, but y'all are gon' have ta wait. I've done my waitin'. I've had my voice taken away, my words silenced and disregarded. Ya'll had your turn. Now the shoe's on the other foot, and y'all are gon' have ta tap them feet and sit in that stink accumulatin'. It's only gon' be worse, so thank ya lucky stars for that. Ya'll got lots of 'em, I reckon. 'Cause y'all are the ones over there. That's proof enough. Ain't it?

Sheeit.

You know I was a smart boy? Top of my class, yessir. Straight As 'cept for the occasional B or two that would sneak in from time ta time. Nobody's perfect, though—am I right? Sir? Can't imagine you did much better than that. Fact, I'd wager you did a whole lot worse than that, 'cause there ain't no way this was your chosen profession. Ha. Sheeit. Bet you wanted ta be a—an astronaut or somethin'. Am I right, sir? Veterinarian? Cowboy? Hell, *I* wanted ta be a cowboy. Then I grew up. Can't *all* be cowboys.

Ma'am? Yes, ma'am—you. I see you brought your child. That's mighty white a' ya, lettin' ya boy see his sister's killer face justice.

Justice. Heh. That's funny.

I see that hate in ya heart, and so I reckon you can see the hate in mine. Birds of a feather, right? Does it not bother you that there ain't no evidence? No, uh, fingerprints? Motive? Modus operandi? Whatnot? No? You just wanna look a man in the eyes and have that man over there tell you the man you lookin' at is the right man. Then maybe you'll get your justice. Don't need ta add up, no. Just need that justice. But ma'am, I don't fully fault you for that. You're a woman in pain. I know that. Pain has a funny way of cloudin' ya senses. So, you hear the right words and see the man they tellin' you is the right man, then that's all you need, 'cause you just want that pain gone. So, ma'am, I sympathize, I do. That's why I'm gon' say this: Whether I'm the *right* man or not, this ain't gon' alleviate nothin'. Maybe you know that, but you're willin' ta give it a shot regardless. 'Cause a' that pain. But your boy, he don't need that hate in ya heart passed down. And that's exactly what you're doin'. Just know that. That's a generational curse you're creatin' taday.

So, I'm gon' say this for the last goddamn time—not ta you, ma'am, not any a' y'all, and certainly not ta you, sir. I'm gon' say it ta you, boy: I did not do it. I did not do what those men tell you I did. And these men ain't cowboys. Hate ta be the one ta tell ya, but, boy, there ain't no cowboys left. Not one. This world went ta Hell in a hand basket long before your time.

Don't you cry, now. One other thing about this *world*: It'll eat you alive if you show it weakness. And I'm not sayin' that showin' tears is showin' weakness, but that's just how the world sees it. I'm tellin' you that 'cause that's somethin' I sure wish my daddy had told me. But he didn't.

Sheeit. Bygones.

See, maybe y'all want me ta say I'm a bad man 'cause my upbringin' made me so, that my daddy molded me into a monster. Ya'll wanna make sense a' things. Sure. But nothin's so cut 'n' dry. Black 'n' white. Never. We *all* in pain though. So, we might never truly see that as fact. Too blinded, stumblin' over this earth in agony. It's a shame, ain't it? Now that'll bring ya tears if you can step back a moment and look at it. But *that* pain. Can't see shit.

Bein' in that cell for as long as I was, it gives ya a long time ta think. About all the moments that lead ta the one ya find yourself in presently. And I tried callin' out to a higher power. I read the Bible. Over and over, I read it, 'til I got papercuts on all my fingers—here, look: you can see 'em right there. That's one more thing I didn't lie about. I reckon if you walked in ta that cell and opened that bible right now, you'd see my blood stainin' the pages. So much so you couldn't even read the words ta Luke 6:37 no more, but that's fine 'cause I got it seared in ta my heart and I'll tell y'all right now what it says beneath that blood: *Do not judge, and YOU will not be judged. Do not condemn, and YOU will not be condemned. Forgive, and YOU will be forgiven.*

Now can I get a *goddamn* AMEN?

Sheeit.

Am I a good man in the eyes of the Lord?

Well, I don't know. But I know He forgives, and so you, sir—you, ma'am—*all a' y'all*: I FORGIVE YOU for your trespasses against ME.

My mind is unclouded and I'm lettin' go a' the pain now. I'm lettin' go a' the hate. I hope you do the same. 'Cause, one day, when I'm absolved—and I promise y'all I WILL be—y'all will have lived ya whole lives with a dark cloud over ya heads, and it won't be until that very moment that y'all will realize the storm was never there ta begin with. 'Cause y'all created that ya'selves.

Yessir.
Yessir, I'm finished.
Nothin' else on my conscience. Not a damn thing.
Go 'head, pull the lever.
I'll see you in Hell or otherwise.
Pull the fuckin' lev—

The Artist

"Here at Captain Bluebeard's Pizzeria, consistency is paramount. Families come to our locations expecting familiarity. The ingredients for all our food are purchased from the same distributor, the menu in our Des Moines restaurant is a carbon copy of the menu in our Boca Raton restaurant. No exceptions. Do you know why that is? Because people don't like change. They want to escape the headlines and nine-to-fives and the hustle and bustle for a couple hours, and they rest easy knowing that, no matter when or where, the moment they step into any of our twenty-five locations, they'll be getting the exact same experience every single time.

"So, it's no coincidence that consistency extends to our aesthetic. Now, you're an artist, and I respect that. Society needs people like you—outside-the-box thinkers and free spirits. Bohemians and such. So, we want to make sure you have fun and get to put your spin on it. But not too much. Not too much fun. Consistency is stability. And stability is important. You understand? Look around you. To the untrained eye, every detail of the wall murals is the same as any other location. But *that's* the beauty of it.

"*You* understand; you're an artist. *You* know. The theme is preplanned and cannot deviate: Nautical. Pirates. Tropical. Erm. Mermaids. *You* see? But *ah*, look here. Come closer. Look: The shade of blue in the Captain's beard? That's more of a cerulean, I'd say. No other location has that shade of blue in the Captain's beard. Not one. That's where you get to really let your artistic side shine. We are all about fun here, after all. And that goes for our Captain Bluebeard's family too. That's what we call our subordinates. We're a business, but we're a *family*. A *family business*. So, what do you say, Pete? Think you're up to it? Would you like to join the Captain Bluebeard's Pizzeria family?"

Pete stared at the man's mouth. Bits of froth had built up at the edges of his lips. He didn't seem to notice or care. Teeth like corroded metal, dripping viscous saliva. Wafting from his body like a demonic aura, layers and layers of cheap cologne battled with the ghost of chain-smoked cigarettes. His fingertips were tinged yellow, and the nails were black, caked with dirt or shit. His words were meaningless and devoid of passion. He showed that himself, in his shoulders, his defeated posture.

He would be dead within a decade and there would be nothing worth noting about his footprint on the world but the sickening and sweet miasma that followed him from room to room. The stench would last longer than the memory of the man. Once a strong breeze passed through, and the stench wiped away, that would be the final echo any person would acknowledge of his existence.

"Yes," said Pete. "When do I start?"

✺   Butte, Montana

"It's Evel, with an 'e'. E-V-E-L. Not Evil." The stripper spoke into the curtain of the private room, her bare back sliding against Pete's chest. "It's like an homage. I'm not into that Satanic stuff. I'm a Christian."

"An homage to what?" Pete held his whiskey away from the woman, contorting himself to take a drink without her gyrations knocking the glass out of his hand. Under the black lights, the maple-tinged liquid appeared purple and luminescent. Even more like a poison.

Evel turned to shoot a glance like he'd sneezed on her. "You must not be from around here."

Her eyes were neon. White and glowing like the pupils had never formed. Everything was black or purple or burning white. The club music hurt his ears and strobe lights scattered colors in beams across the ceiling like gunfire through night-vision goggles. The overstimulation manifested as a heavy stone of nausea at the center of his stomach.

"No. I'm here on business."

"Business? Shit, there ain't much business to be done here. What kinda work you in?"

"History."

"Listerine?"

"HISTORY. I'm a historian."

"Oh, got it. Got it. You gotta speak up in here, honey. What kinda history?"

"Death. The history of death. You know about the Speculator Mine disaster?"

The song ended. Before Evel could ask, Pete handed her more money. She stuffed it into her G-string, sat down in the booth beside him, and reached into her high heel boot to retrieve the small plastic baggie. "Shit yeah, everybody here knows about that. How you know that, and you don't know Evel Knievel was born here?" She poured out some of the white powder on the table, separated two uneven lines with the end of her sharpened fake nail, and snorted the longest of the couple with a rolled-up dollar before handing it to Pete.

Pete inhaled the coke and threw back his head, blunting the rush with a sip of liquor. "'Cause he didn't die here." He could immediately feel his heart screaming, his blood vibrating. He wanted to spill it onto the table and see if it sang to him. "Out of all the ways he could have died, he went out like anyone else. He had an unextraordinary death. It cheapened his life's work."

"I wouldn't talk like that around here."

Pete rubbed his nose with the back of his hand and blood leaked onto his knuckle. It gleamed like a star system beneath the black lights. "Who gives a fuck—Those miners had a beautiful death. Choking on smoke, lit up by a sea of fire. Trapped together. 168 trapped, engulfed rats. That's a death worth living for. A shared, final exhalation."

"What's that, baby?" Evel was preoccupied with separating more lines, like a child organizing M&Ms by color.

"Nothing. I feel sick."

"What kinda sick? Like sleepy? Or is your jaw all tight?"

Pete massaged his chin, digging his bloodied knuckle into the grooves of his molars. "Second one."

"That's good. Everything you get here is either cut with crank or fentanyl. If you're grinding your teeth, that means I bought the shit that won't kill you."

"I need something that will slow me back down. It's too loud in here. There's too much happening."

Evel kept snorting the laced drug. "I don't have anything like that on me."

"I do," said Pete. "At my hotel." He stared at the crucifix dangling between Evel's breasts. "Out of any image people like you could have chosen, you picked the circumstances of his death.

That's how it all began. A death so perfect, it changed the world. He was in so much pain. So much agony—that it became art."

The cross glinted black like a diamond at the bottom of an oil spill. It was beautiful. It was everything to which he aspired. His inspiration. He reached out to touch the necklace.

"The fuck you think you're doing?" Evel slapped his hand away, the white powder mixing with blood, caking around her nostril to appear crystalline. Everything about her shimmered. A still life, incomplete.

"How much do I need to pay you to leave with me?"

"Fuck that. You're fuckin' weird, dude. Time's up." Evel gummed what remained on the table, stood, and disappeared behind the curtain.

Rivulets of crimson across the brim of his cap. Deep blue clashing with olive greens, forcing movement in the sea's waves. Thin brushstrokes of black and brown, shadows inside the pockets of his eyes, the sun-struck skin revealing his age and demeanor. He's lost. He's been lost, searching for a treasure that will fill the hole in his heart. Nothing had come, and in the blood-red veins protruding from the whites of his eyes, the burden of this knowledge weighed heavy on his soul. He was tired but couldn't show the crew. They'd felt his weakness for months on the open ocean. Murmurs of mutiny echoed beneath the hull in the dead of night, in between emptied bottles of pilfered rum.

Their faces were obscured by the glaring orange light of the western sun, their scimitars glinting gold, faint tinges of crusted black blood along the serrated edges and at the bottoms of hilts, where heads had caved in beneath their mercy. The woman of wood stood at the mast, arms out towards the promise of better tomorrows, of plunder and sex and alcohol and tropical fruits on the shores of an untapped island. Her tail a vision of turquoise chipped tan by the whitewash of gale winds and waves, purple barnacles attached unnaturally to hide her supple oak breasts that the crew so yearned to be real after days and days of hallucinations, scurvy, and isolation.

Indiscernible grays and dull bronze lingered just beneath the water's surface, a hint at the reality that the volatile depths may as well have been a desert at the horn of Africa, a place they once knew well and celebrated when it proved to be a bounty of proportions they seldom ever seen and may never see again. Hope born from exhaustion and decay. Exploration intermingling with the agony of a vast and empty landscape. Beauty in death, and death in a life untapped. Damned if you do and damned if you don't. But you have to, the Captain said in the crease of his brow, the determined emerald green in his eyes that shimmered as they stared out towards possibilities both limitless and void.

"You know what you should do? Add a parrot on Bluebeard's shoulder. Kids will love that." The man stood an inch behind him, breath warm on the nape of his neck.

Pete felt the overwhelming urge to stab the paintbrush into his right eyeball. "I need to be alone when I work. I'll let you know when it's finished."

The man leaned over his shoulder as if about to lay his chin down upon it like a cooing lover. "And maybe make him smile. Captain Bluebeard's Pizzeria—it's a happy place. Happy. He looks depressed. Can you fix that? A big smile." Miming a grin, the man grimaced like a child taking his 2nd grade picture. A layer of yellow plaque coated his two front teeth. "Oh! You know what else you could do? Give him a gold tooth. They'll love that. A big smile with a gold tooth."

Pete swallowed the rage like bile, refusing to turn away from his artwork. "I will let you know when it's finished."

The sound of wet smacks penetrated his ears each time the man spoke: "Right. Of course. You, uh—I'll let you get back to it."

The footsteps grew quieter across the plastic tarp until disappearing behind the latching and locking of the office door.

Pete closed his eyes and exhaled. Again. Exhale. Again.

He stepped back and looked at his creation. It was an abomination. Something was missing.

Its heart beat through dried veins.

 Pine Bluff, Arkansas

"The FBI estimates there are twenty-five to fifty serial killers operating in the United States at any given time. Odds are you have a friend who was—or will be—killed by one. Drifters tend to target sex workers."

Mercedes the stripper stared with her mouth agape as Pete told her this. He gave off the energy of someone not worth the money, and his words were that of a predator, but since being knocked down to weekday afternoon shifts at The Devil's Den, she was desperate for income. The owner, Manuel, had upped her fee to perform by $75 when she refused him sexual favors. Each minute that passed without pulling coins from Pete's lizard brain was more money she would owe Manuel simply for being there.

"Why do you know things like that?" she asked. He'd bought her a vodka-cranberry, and she drank deep to separate herself from her pulsating survival instinct. If he could afford to buy her a drink, he could afford a lap dance.

"Because I'm the guy who came up with the statistic." He held out a hand. "Special Agent Peter M. I can't give you my last name. National security—you understand."

Mercedes pulled away, the sweat that coated his palm glistening across hers. "We're even then. I can't tell you mine either. Personal security." She pivoted and scanned the strip club. Karma was asleep on the pool table with a glass in her hand, her half-naked form bathed in darkness but backlit by the sun creeping in through the crack in the bolted front door.

Pete turned to see what distracted Mercedes and was struck with unspeakable inspiration. It was like witnessing Pythia collapse and seize at the Temple of Delphi. She was the image of a lost Edward Hopper painting. Genius. Remarkable. "Who is that?"

She was going to lose him. "That's just Karma. She's fine." Mercedes faced Pete with exaggerated bedroom eyes and slid her hand across his thigh. "How about a dance?"

"She doesn't seem fine." He couldn't look away. The image was arresting. The seed of something beautiful waiting to bloom. To be molded into a masterpiece. "I'm gonna check on her."

Pete stood and Mercedes felt the money slipping through her fingers. Another lost day.

"Hey." Pete shook the woman until she opened her eyes.

Brilliant shades of turquoise held together by a rim of auburn-gold.

"Do you need help?"

Karma stirred and sat up on the pool table. "Mmmm. Nope. I'm fine, baby." She watched his face sink into the shadows as he realized her long red hair was a wig. "You want me?"

"Yes. But not here."

"What you mean?"

"I have ten grand if you come back with me to my hotel."

"Shit, you must think I'm stupid."

Pete reached into his pocket and showed the green edges of the concealed lump of bills. "I can give you five now. Five after."

Her eyes widened and became glittering crystal balls. "Aite. Fine. Not here though, put that away. I'll go out the back and meet you in the parking lot."

As they drove, Pete watched her through the corner of his eye. It was all a trick of the lighting. Outside, the image faded. As if a marble statue had turned to dust once introduced to the sun. "Your wig is poor quality. You should take better care with how you present yourself."

Karma didn't care what the stranger had to say. She held the wad of cash tight in her fist, hidden away within her jacket pocket. Five now, five later. He'd made good on the deal so far.

"I feel duped, you know. I thought it was real." Pete reached into the mess of sunburst-red locks. "I'll still pay ten. But I might not have if I'd known."

The inspiration was fading from his mind, the spark that had been lit at the sight of her perfectly framed body was flickering in the winds of uncertainty, but he was a professional. He would work with what he had. Any medium, any tools—a professional can create with nothing, if need be.

Karma remained silent, looking out the window to watch the neighborhoods regress into disrepair and poverty the farther they went.

"This town is a shithole." Pete flourished a hand across the windshield. "I read you have one of the worst crime rates in the country. Unsolved murders and disappearances every day. There's no need to be creative here. Unextraordinary places breed unextraordinary acts. There's no reason to take pride in what you do when the place you live gives you no inspiration to try. That's no way to live."

The car turned and slowed inside the lot of a Motel 8. Pete parked and looked into Karma's eyes as if appraising a gem. "I think you'll be different though. What I saw in you—I'm never wrong about these things. I have an eye for it."

They walked into the single-bed room. Beer bottles and paint supplies littered the carpet. Beyond that, Karma could make out few other details through the lone, hospital-yellow florescent light and drawn blinds.

She sat down on the bed. "Are you a talent agent or somethin'?"

Pete opened the mini-fridge and pulled out two beers, popping off the caps using the rim of the center table. "No." He handed her the bottle and took a long pull from his own. They sat on the bed in silence until he reached out and brushed his fingers along her leg. "This lighting is a detriment, but I was right. I can see it." He traced the blue veins running up her calves, feeling the goose bumps and thin hairs rise upon his touch. "I almost...hear it. Can you?"

Karma froze, trying to swallow her rapid heartbeat. It felt like a bad dream. That was it. Just a bad dream. She wanted to move away but the accumulating fear acted as a form of hypnosis. She was out of body. "Hear what?"

Pete leaned in closer, pressing his ear against her chest. *Exhaling. Inhaling. Exhaling.* "A symphony."

The moment she pulled away, Pete leapt on top of her. His hand squeezing her throat, he could feel the firmness of the trachea, and, through the choked grunts, she tried to scream.

He brandished the knife concealed in his jacket and plunged it into her chest like a stake through a vampire's heart.

A spurt of blood launched onto his face when the knife dislodged. Pollock unleashing the first brushstroke upon a clean canvas. It was warm on his face and her eyes bulged and it was so beautiful, it was so beautiful.

The blood leaked down her chest and it vibrated and then he heard them—he heard the first notes. Faint, distant, but they echoed, beckoned to be let free and sing.

She slapped away his hand, but he smiled so wide, the sound drowned out her scream and he stabbed again, in the stomach—again, and the blood pooled and poured and it was so red. it gleamed under the light, and it grew. It grew from one note to two, from a section of violins to woodwinds melding together and they sang. They sang!

The room was alive, and she was dying, and the blood shook the earth beneath the bed, and she screamed and screamed, and Pete smiled, and Pete laughed, and he said, "Do you hear it? I was right about you! You're magnificent!" And the orchestra bloomed and created acoustics in pockets of empty air as if the hotel had become a grand arena, and each note touched the next, and they swirled into a crescendo, and Pete was the conductor, Pete was the conductor, the knife his wand, and she shouted again, drowned out by the masterpiece that came forth from her wounds, but still the words were there and he heard: "PLEASE. PLEASE. PLEASE. I DON'T WANNA DIE. WHO ARE YOU?"

And Pete could no longer contain his euphoria for he knew what song she played with the organs within her body that spilled bloody chords, angelic and harmonious, and it was Mozart, it was "Mozart's Symphony No. 41," and how perfect it was, how perfect it was that it was the master's final piece ever created, and Pete listened and crooned and swayed and grinned, and he stabbed again, again, again, and the screams became lilting flutes, and the blood covered his body and hers as if they together had been born anew, and spurned by the perfection, and reminded of her final ask, he cried out with pleasure: "I'M A FUCKING ARTIST," and the knife, the conductor's wand, the instrument of death and rebirth, sliced her throat from ear to ear.

Tragedy had struck. The crew had been at sea for eleven months, steered into the deepest reaches of the ocean, in the center of an apocalyptic storm. The sky was black, jet-black. They hadn't seen the sun. They'd forgotten the feeling of natural warmth on their skin. The stars were choked and dead behind the veil of ash and sulfur and clouds like the omnipotent, expansive eye of a demon. Food and rum and drinking water ran dry far too long ago. The days melded into a seamless and unending nightmare. The crew drew straws. An unnamed deckhand chose the shortest. The captain watched the ocean swell and become darker and darker to match the sky, unable to face what'd become of the boy. He had chosen to starve and die with what little strength and dignity that remained. His skin was ashen and his lips scarred with scrapes that never healed after dehydration peeled away the soft layer of once healthy pink.

Behind him, it was happening: The final feast. *Take this and eat it, my flesh and blood.* The men knelt in a circle, dipping hands into the boy's open stomach, pulling his entrails and sucking out the blood and flesh, their hands stained crimson, crimson, crimson, their mouths dripping like feral dogs, their eyes black, their pupils dilated until humanity no longer exists within. Like buzzards, they ate and drank and knelt and growled as they fought over the best pieces of raw meat.

Crimson, crimson, crimson. It glittered and sang and howled and it was the ingredient that'd been missing all along. She helped create a masterpiece. It dried black and coagulated unlike the rest of the paint, but it sang. The mural awakened and you heard the men grunt, and you heard the snapping of bones and the sucking of marrow, and the symphony played to the rhythm of the boy's still-beating heart. His mouth was agape as if screaming but he made no sound, shock strangling his throat like the hand of God. The emerald eyes were held open by morbid curiosity, gazing down in removed fascination at the mutilated and exposed innards. In his mind, he floated through the ashes, a moment of divine clarity achieved through final, supreme horror.

Pete dipped his brush into the bucket of her offering and hurled the blood across the scene, again, again, crimson, crimson, crimson. It was everywhere, washing the deck and staining the wood, and, even when the great wave finally struck, and the ship sunk to the ocean floor, the stains would remain for they could not be undone. What the men did could never be undone, and so they ate and drank, and the captain watched the horizon like staring into the abyss, but the abyss stared back only in the hearts of the crew.

Genius. It was fucking genius.

Pete stepped back and looked in awe at his creation, swaying and humming to the music it played for him, that she played for him. He turned and briefly pitied the man who lay dead upon the plastic tarp in the empty restaurant. Pete pitied him not for his death, but for his inability to behold what he made. But the audience would come.

Soon, they would all see his genius. And they would marvel at the work. There was still one more to finish. His greatest piece yet. A beautiful finale.

A twinge of guilt tugged at Pete's chest. He stared at the man's body and sighed. "For you," he said, and washed his brush, dipped it into the cerulean acrylic paint, and put the finishing touch to his canvas.

His fucking beard was blue.

꙳   **Peoria, Arizona**

"He told me his name was Peter. That he worked for the FBI or something. She left with him, and that was the last time I heard from her. I don't know anything else about him."

Pete watched Mercedes speak on the television as he sat drinking at The Bloated Fish Tavern. She wore civilian clothes and looked as though she'd been crying.

The reporter feigned professional horror and turned to the camera: "Two days ago, the body of Carmella Roosevelt was found in a Motel 8 in Pine Bluff, Arkansas, paid for in cash by a man named Ralph Hodges. Authorities tell us this is a fake name, and that he is presumed armed and dangerous. The FBI and Arkansas State Police are offering a $10,000 reward for anyone who has information on the identity or current whereabouts of the suspect. The FBI also denies any knowledge of a man matching the suspect's description working for the Bureau."

"They're leaving out the best part," he mumbled. "Hey, turn it up, will ya?"

The bartender obliged and pivoted to see what Pete was so interested in.

"We've gotten unconfirmed reports that the body was found drained of blood and staged in some kind of sacrilegious position. Authorities have not ruled out the possibility that this was the work of...a Satanic cult. Chilling stuff. Back to you, Jim."

"Thanks, Jennifer. Awful. Just awful. In other news, the Cardinals snagged their first victory of the season with—"

Pete scoffed, and let the whiskey cool the flames spreading in his gut. "Satanic cult. What a load of shit." He swiveled around in his barstool after realizing no one was listening. "People are scared to recognize art when they see it."

The bartender eyed him before looking away, letting the television blare to drown out the stranger. There were a dozen creeps like Pete in the bar on any given day. Ugly, manic faces with ugly, manic souls. He just poured their drinks and let them talk to themselves. He left people like him alone.

"These days, you have to fucking spell it out for 'em. You gotta spoon-feed everything to these idiots. They don't recognize genius when it's staring them right in the fuckin' eyes."

As he said this, Jennifer reappeared on the screen with a bright red banner across the bottom: ***BREAKING NEWS***. "Sorry, Jim, but I'm getting word now that another body has been found in Pine Bluff. Details are scarce but authorities are already connecting this to the murder of Carmella Roosevelt. At the scene, a massive, disturbing mural was found painted on the wall. This building was slated to become a new Captain Bluebeard's Pizzeria, and we're hearing that the only two people who were given access to the unfinished restaurant were the victim and a freelance painter commissioned by the company named Peter Mahoney. So far, the beloved national restaurant chain has issued no official statement. Make sure to stay tuned, as we'll be bringing you live updates as they come in. Again, if you have any information regarding Peter Mahoney, the FBI is urging citizens to—"

Pete stood, threw twenty dollars on the bar, and walked outside.

"Disturbing? Fuck. Shit. Fuck you, *disturbing*. Gotta fucking spell it out for 'em. Idiots. Dumb it down, clean it up, always gotta make it accessible. Fuck you, *accessible*. I'm a fucking artist. 'It's cerulean, Pete.' Fucking *cerulean*. Christ."

He weaved across congested roads, blowing through red lights as loose paint supplies and a black canvas bag bounced across the backseat of his car like rocks in a tumbler. There wasn't much time, but it wouldn't take long.

It wouldn't take long at all.

Great art didn't have to take time; it needed to make a statement, and Pete's statement would be succinct. A single note would elicit the same response as a full concerto, if played to perfection. One drop of oil can pollute an entire ocean. *It can be done. It can be done.*

The car careened into a lamppost guarding the entrance to the building. Pete opened the mangled door and spilled onto the concrete with the canvas bag over his shoulder, pulling shards of glass from his arms. Under the yellow light, the glass twinkled and the blood came, warm and red, and ran down his limbs like raindrops, and the notes played—dim, muffled, but they played, and he knew.

He knew it was to be his defining piece. His sliver of immortality.

Stepping inside the cavernous space already lined with plastic tarp and walled by thick, dull plaster, Pete felt as if he'd entered the hollow soul of a dead giant. The blood dripped from his arms and became life, like flowers sprouting from salted earth.

"I called the cops! You just—you stay away from me, alright?"

Pete turned and saw a man standing rigid against the far corner. He hadn't even noticed. The man was wallpaper, without soul, nothing more than another imperfection in the lifeless environment. An abandoned universe of empty matter. "Hey. I'm supposed to talk to you," said Pete. "I'm the artist."

"I know who you are! You're a criminal! Don't come any closer!"

Pete stared at the man's eyes, searching for fire, and proved his assumption. "You don't know what you're missing. I see it, though. You're missing a piece."

"What?" The man remained planted to the floor as Pete walked towards him. A single horrifying glimpse of divinity. The closest he would ever come.

The knife plunged through his left ear; its blade buried inside his head.

The man collapsed.

Blood spurted from the hilt like water from a clogged faucet. There was no sound but the soft gurgling at the back of his throat. No music. Not one note.

It was the saddest thing Pete had ever seen.

He hoped that final glimpse had lasted longer in the man's mind than it had in the room. He hoped it carried over into the last synaptic flashes and became an eternity. For a moment, he really did.

Then came the sirens. One turned to two.

And two turned to many.

That's okay. There's still time.

Pete zipped open the canvas bag and pulled out his tools. He stepped towards the blank wall, crimson dripping close behind like scattered inkblots.

Terrible excitement blended with fear, and born from the adrenaline it created, Pete felt the need to speak, and what he said was this: "Maybe it's too on the nose."

But as he placed the back of his right hand against the wall, and the sirens grew loud and close, and their lights burned blue and red behind the windows, and the trail of blood played mournful, solitary notes like a dying maestro's final concert, and he stabbed the first rusted nail through his palm, and he raised the hammer high above his head, Pete thought,

Nah. They still won't get it.

Worm Food

"I heard when your head's cut off, you still have thirty seconds of consciousness before the brain dies. You just sit there with no body, blinking for half a minute." Danny prodded the severed head with his boot. "There's this account of some guy executed by the guillotine. While his head was in the little basket, someone said his name and his eyes opened, and he looked at the person who called him. He recognized his name."

Terrance danced around the pool of blood and reached into the body's pants pocket. He opened the wallet and looked at the driver's license. "Hey. Hey, Mary? Mary! Wake up!" He whistled like commanding a dog to heel. "Right here. Hello."

Together, they stared at the head. Danny frowned. "Maybe it doesn't always work." He surveyed the wreckage of the car crash: the shattered windows, the twisted metal, the skid marks, the caustic smell of skin and fat tissue fusing into leather seats. A solitary arm protruded from a jagged hole in the other car's windshield, erect and rigid as if it were waving at them. The rest of its body had flown through the open passenger window and disappeared somewhere in the cornfield on the side of the road. Physics was interesting like that.

"I think it needs to be a clean cut," said Terrance. He watched the blood and brain matter ooze from the eyes and nostrils. "She got bounced around too much. Damaged the brain stem. I bet that's what it is."

"Yeah. Maybe," Danny answered. "If she'd worn a seatbelt, it might have sliced right through."

"Maybe. She'd had to have been going pretty fast though."

"Yeah."

The men took turns frowning at Mary's unblinking head.

Well," Terrance sighed, putting a cigarette to his lips. "Let's write it up. Cops'll be here soon."

"The experiment was bullshit. And MacDougall was a sadist. I thought we were trying to do something real here."

Danny looked out onto miles of flat farmland as Terrance drove towards a three-car pileup along Route 66. The call had just come in over the police scanner, but it was a remote location, and they were close, so the two men figured they'd have at least a five- or six-minute window to observe before authorities arrived.

"We are. And he was, too. Science isn't always gonna be pretty, Danny. Sometimes you have to get comfortable with a moral gray area to find progress."

"I don't care so much about the morality, okay? It was mostly for argument's sake."

"We're not arguing. We're having a discussion. Why was it bullshit? I wanna know why you think it was bullshit."

Danny waved at a herd of black-and-white cows grazing by the highway. "His whole deal began with the idea that animals don't even have souls. That's a presumptuous baseline. And how do you think he got the dogs? They didn't come in dying. He didn't just walk into a pet shelter and go, 'Hey. I need to kill some dogs. Can I have some dogs that are already on their way out?' He poisoned healthy strays, strapping 'em to the table to measure the weight. That's sadism. That's sick, man."

Terrance was half-listening, his eyes narrowed on the road ahead, waiting for a glimmer of broken glass or a plume of smoke. "Okay, but that has nothing to do with whether the results were bullshit. Be objective, Danny. Put on your fuckin' big boy pants and be scientific about this. Where'd the 21 grams go?"

"Well, first of all, none of that was conclusive. One patient lost weight at death but then lost even more weight. Another lost weight but gained the weight back. And he didn't even really bother to weigh the dogs properly at all. His mind was already made up before then: Animals don't have souls. That's bias. That alone should disregard the experiment entirely."

"But the third patient—"

"21.3 grams, yeah. But that could be anything. The organs are shutting down, sweat glands are opening up. It could have easily been 21 grams of sweat. He could have shit himself a little. There are lots of explanations. And there was no follow-up. No repeating of the experiment for a better conclusion. The guy was a hack and a fucking sadist."

"You just don't like that he hurt animals. That's bias, too. You're still not being objective."

Danny followed a scattered group of sheep with his eyes. They were like little isolated bubbles of fog hovering over the field. "I'm *objectively* saying fuck that guy. We'll get better results—on people."

Terrance eyed his partner, gauging his mood before answering: "I'm just playing devil's advocate. You don't need to start fuckin' crying."

"I'm not." Danny squinted and pointed to a distant spot on the road. "There. Look."

Three cars sat smoldering across both lanes, crumpled into each other like a defective accordion. The middle car had the worst of it: A bright orange fire over the hood hissed and flickered in the wind. The windshield of the front car had been blown out and a streak of blood led to a body lying flat on the asphalt. The car at the back, presumably the instigating party, was still running, its engine revving like the driver was in shock and still pressing down on the gas pedal.

Terrance pulled to the side of the road. "Alright. Let's see what we can get. In and out—five minutes."

They approached the backmost car. Its tires were squealing, unable to propel farther into the trunk of its roadblock. The sweet smell of burning rubber floated from the scene.

Danny pressed his face against the driver's window. The man was slumped over the steering wheel, his mouth agape, his eyes glazed over. Dribbles of blood ran down his temple. "It's deadweight," he said. "His foot's stuck like a cement block on the pedal. He's long gone."

Terrance grunted. "Alright, next one then. Let's go, c'mon."

The center car's back half had been crushed up to the center console like a turtle retreating into its shell. The woman inside was mangled beyond recognition, her head caved in and body twisted into an inhuman shape as if stuffed into a small box. Her arms and legs were shattered and bent in different directions across her chest.

"Don't bother," said Terrance. "She's a fuckin' pretzel. Next one."

Danny pointed to the third body lying a few yards away from the accident and whistled. It had been thrown through the windshield upon impact. "That boy grew wings. Goddamn." He jogged ahead while Terrance lingered at the woman's corpse, mumbling something about the circus and contortionism.

Danny took a knee next to the man and, upon seeing that he was still breathing, felt his heartrate spike. "Hey. Hey, man." He shook the victim's shoulder—the one that wasn't relinquished of clothes and skin from skidding across the road—and he looked at Danny as if he were gazing up at an angel.

"Help me," he said. Blood poured over his broken teeth. Blood too drained from his left ear, so Danny knew hemorrhaging would cloud his mind soon, and death would quickly follow.

"*Three minutes,*" Terrance called over, his eyes still trained on the mess of skin, flesh, and bone wedged between the center car's seat and dashboard. "We got a live one or what?"

He was a perfect candidate. They'd never found someone so within that sweet spot between life and death. Danny fumbled his words when yelling over his shoulder, still staring into the man's eyes, watching the lights dim. "*Y—yeah. Hang on. Just hang on.*" He grabbed the man's chin, ignoring his plea. "Hey. Hey, focus. Look at me. What do you see right now?"

The man's expression was blank. He was in shock, or in awe, or too muddled to make sense of the situation. It was possible they'd missed the threshold where he could comprehend language. But, in a choked whisper, the man said, "Help me."

"Yeah, yeah. Yeah, I'm gonna help you. You're gonna be fine. But you need to tell me what's going on. You're dying right now. I need you to understand that and tell me what you're experiencing. Quickly now."

Danny realized he was leaning hard against the man's chest because when his heart stopped, the hollowness reverberated against his arm.

The man's eyes opened wide. As if something had appeared. He inhaled and failed to let go of the breath within his lungs, as if he knew it was his last and refused the finality. The man extended a limp and broken arm to Danny's cheek and leaned close to his ear. The words he spoke left his mouth with the exhale, and after Danny fell backwards upon hearing them, it was no longer a man who had spoken, but an empty body.

Terrance appeared from behind, peering at the corpse. "Did you get anything? Looked like he was wriggling around a bit. I figured he was too banged up, though."

Danny turned around, hunched, sitting there at the center of the road, his stunned and pale face a vivid reflection of what he'd witnessed.

"Goddamn." Terrance grinned and laughed. "You look like you've seen a ghost."

When driving at night in the middle of nowhere, the streetlamps few and far between, the new moon hanging in the sky, you could begin to feel as though they're not moving at all. The world was veiled by darkness and fog, and the only sign you were alive was the passage of yellow lines appearing at the dim end of your headlights, until disappearing again beneath the wheels. It began to feel like purgatory, like the illusion of movement, traveling nowhere forever.

Danny hadn't talked since they got back in the car. The words played in his head, attaching to every thought like roots of a poisonous plant.

"I didn't think you were this squeamish." Terrance had grown tired of the silence. "You've seen worse. You'll see worse. I thought we were in this together."

Danny remained stoic. Trance-like. Watching the yellow lines appear and disappear in the claustrophobic new world of fog and darkness. "We are," he answered. "We need more data."

"Did you get anything from the guy? You didn't write anything down. It's important we write everything down, even if it's not directly related to our hypothesis. We need to do this right. Okay? You gotta stay with me here. Don't get all loopy 'cause you saw a dead body."

"I'm not loopy," said Danny. "He was too far gone. Didn't know what he was saying. Nothing worth writing down. Worthless babble. That's all."

Terrance appraised his partner with a brief glance. "What did he tell you?"

"Gibberish. Just gibberish."

"Did you stick to the script?"

"Yes, man. I stuck to the fuckin' script. We just need more data. I need to talk to more people. We're moving too slowly. Our methods aren't conducive to—"

"Our methods are sound," Terrance interrupted. "We can't rush this. We gotta do this by the book."

"What fuckin' book?"

"It's a figure of speech. We can't let our own ideologies muddy the results. You need to be objective, Danny. Tell me what he said to you. Whatever it was obviously shook you up. I can't have you crashing this whole thing because a dying man with head trauma told you he saw the Devil or some shit. People are fucked up, they're gonna see a lotta different things. That's not what we're after here."

"Okay." Danny turned and glared into the side of Terrance's head. "Then what are we after? Huh? What do you think we're gonna find? And what happens if it's something you don't wanna know?" When Terrance didn't respond, he repeated, "I need more data. Another subject."

Danny turned on the police scanner. He flipped between channels of white noise and minor infraction codes before an emergency responder rambled off a description and address in a monotone voice that clashed with the event's circumstances. "How close are we?"

Terrance whipped his head between Danny and the scanner's blue glow. "What—now? Are you kidding? We don't do that. I won't. Car crashes and medical emergencies, no blatant crimes. That's the rule."

Danny ignored this and reiterated: "How close, Terrance?"

Terrance looked for a street sign but didn't answer.

"What happened to being objective? This is prime. This is what we want."

"*Objective?*" Terrance snapped, his knuckles turning white against the wheel. "I could ask you the same fuckin' thing. That guy got you rattled. You're in no shape right now. And it's not close enough, alright? It'd be a mistake."

"Fine, then you get me nearby and drop me off. I'll observe by myself. Do both our jobs."

"You understand what you're asking me? You really wanna run that risk?"

"Yes, motherfucker." Danny tapped on the police scanner. "Clock's tickin'. You want the data or not? No—look at me. You want an answer?"

Terrance's eyes shifted between Danny and the rearview mirror, mumbling to himself before abruptly pulling a U-turn. "Hang on," he said. "We're gonna have to break a few laws."

The engine screamed as they disappeared farther into the nebulous fog, the highway's yellow lines the sole guide leading them through oblivion.

The front door had been left open. The lights of the all the surrounding houses were on, and a neighbor's dog was barking as if trying to warn Danny of what waited inside. There was no time, he accepted that. It didn't matter. Nothing else mattered but the words seared into his mind.

"In and out," said Terrance. "I mean it. I'll circle the block and you meet me outside in two minutes. Hey—" He snapped his fingers to get Danny's attention. "You hear me?"

"Yeah." He stepped out of the car and watched it disappear into the shadows beneath glowing streetlamps.

The door was blocked on the other side, stopping halfway with a soft *thud*. Danny squeezed through the space and found the body of a man. It was splayed across the welcome mat, its arms out. Like so many others, its mouth was agape, as if his final breath expelled with a scream. The pool of blood was still spreading across the hardwood floor, pouring from a small wound in its back. Its eyes were blue and milky with tears. The blood and the body were still warm. The man was very dead.

Across the room, a dog sat whining on its haunches, wagging its tail, its ears pinned back in fear or confusion. Beside the dog lay the woman. Somewhere far enough away outside, the sound of police sirens approached. Danny carefully stepped forward, holding out the back of his hand towards the dog. He kneeled beside the woman. She'd missed the brain and had blown off the lower half of her jaw. Her tongue hung loosely through the hole in her face, resting atop the row of exposed bottom teeth. Her breathing was ragged and shallow, and her eyes followed Danny as he observed what she'd become. A nauseous mixture of blood-choked gurgles and hoarse squeals escaped her throat, and nothing more. The revolver lay beside her limp right hand. Its barrel was still hot to the touch.

"Hi," said Danny. He reached out to stroke the dog's head, and it leaned in closer, desperately needing comfort, whining but not barking. He wanted to take the dog away but knew it wouldn't yet leave. His empathy was reserved for the animal, and the empathy and worry it had for the woman was all she would receive. It was going to be a drawn-out death. Slow and painful.

"I'm going to ask you some questions," he said as calmly as he could. "You are dying. You may already know this. Or you may think that you will be saved. You will not. I need you to understand that fact before you answer the questions. Do you understand what I'm telling you?"

The woman's eyes grew large, and her breathing became rapid and panicked. She formed the words that were still discernable but slurred as if spoken by a stroke victim: "Help me."

"I will," Danny replied. "First, answer this question. Knowing what you now know, tell me what you see. Tell me what you're experiencing. Think very carefully about this. Banish the idea of God or an afterlife or the actions of your past. Your answer requires objectivity. It will be the most important answer you will ever give. It will be your salvation—the truth."

Allowing the woman time to stare and scream inside her mind, Danny stroked the dog's head, kneading its ears. He took its collar in his hand and looked at the tag: "Charlie. Hi, Charlie. Good boy. You're a good boy."

Saliva and blood pooled beneath her tongue and spilled over her bottom lip. The sirens grew louder. A car screeched to a stop just outside the house.

"You're running out of time," he urged. "Quickly."

Terrance slammed the door against the body while trying to get in. "We gotta go," he shouted, and gazed down at the corpse, and at Danny kneeling before the woman.

Danny didn't turn, but continued staring into the woman's eyes, waiting. The distant glare of red and blue lights shined through the windows.

"Just leave her! Fuck it, man! C'mon!"

"Do you wanna hear something?" Danny whispered into her ear as Terrance grasped the back of his shirt. "I'll tell you what I know. But it doesn't have to be true. Remember that. It doesn't have to be." He plucked the dead man's words from his mind, tearing each consonant and vowel off the walls as if they'd been stapled to the inside of his skull, fighting every instinct that howled for him to hide them away, and spoke softly, so softly, for only the woman to hear.

Her eyes turned to fire. Resurrected but for a moment. Unspeakable horror erupted from every nerve, and she so desperately tried to scream, but what came was something unearthly. Not evil but a response to it. Blood drained from her face, her hair graying before his eyes, the skin melting away under the weight of revelatory visions. As if he had spoken the forbidden phrase to call upon the end of the world.

With such a force that betrayed her frailty, the woman clasped both sides of Danny's head, thrusting him towards her. There were screams and movement, and the room exploded with lights and life, but the woman spoke into his ear, and in that moment, they were forever locked together, separate from the repercussions of any action, of history and time itself. Burrowed together beneath infinity, the woman spoke. The pieces of the universe unraveled like thin yarn. And Danny heard.

His mind shattered. Every perceived belief and moral and justification that made him who he had become—hoarded and protected across a lifetime by the certainty of self—unfurled and dissolved. It was truth. The sequence of sounds uttered only once before, or only heard once before, and it was true. It was true. It was true.

He had made a terrible mistake.

A different pair of hands, larger and gloved, pulled him by the collar. The revolver was in Danny's hand, and it fired.

The policeman fell.

Another, and the sounds of Hell turned to the swan song of dying cells. Ringing.

But still the words were there.

The next man fell. A molten hot force struck his shoulder, and still it was nothing, it felt like nothing, not numbness, but something further within the abyss of that which should never be known.

It had all been rendered meaningless. There was nothing.

Danny stood. The two policemen lay bleeding out, coughing, and Terrance lay on his stomach, handcuffed, and he said words, but they were not the words of the woman, and so they were without sound.

He aimed the pistol and fired, and it struck his partner in the head, and he turned to the woman, the oracle, the demon, or that which had instantaneously and briefly inhabited one, aimed, and fired.

He collapsed on the ground, pressed the hot barrel against his temple, inhaling the scent of cauterizing flesh, and pulled the trigger. And, at the moment, he heard the dull *click*, the words that swirled and became him like a cancer overtaking every cell, every molecule, rearranged before his eyes like a fantastic lightshow, and it was so funny. It was so fucking funny. The words burned through his eyes like a brand thrust into the cow, and it was—it was the greatest fucking joke he'd ever heard.

The revolver dropped beside the oracle's corpse. Danny leaned against the dog, still waiting, still whining, and wrapped his arms around the animal as more and more sirens erupted across the night sky. He squeezed the dog, burying his face into its warm fur, and the tears dried, his mind as emptied as the handgun.

"You're a good boy," he said. "Good, lucky boy. Lucky, lucky boy, Charlie."

The dog slid out from between his clenched arms, glanced around at the hollow bodies, and stepped through the door, into the cool evening air.

Danny didn't protest, didn't call out, didn't claw the floor in vain for its return.

"That's a good boy," he repeated, letting the poison settle. A grin pulled across his face by the hands of unknowable certainty. "Lucky boy."

The Utopian Mask

They don't scream like we do.

Pleasure-howls that twist around walls and bleed through the cracks underneath locked doors. Yips that crash into the echoes they create like shattering mirrors. They submerge our voices until we can't hear our own kind through the bars and barbed wires that separate us. Their enjoyment is louder than our pain that brings it about.

I hate them. I hate them and I want them to know but communicating that would only increase the volume of their satisfaction.

I know what they do here. They segregate us and they trick us with their actions and their metal curtains and pleasure-howls. They hide what they do until it's our time to join what lies on the other side, but I know what they do here. They placate us with stimuli and exhaustion, our eyes too tired to see farther than our own bodies pressed against each other, our stomachs too empty and riddled with ulcers to anticipate the pain that's greater than what we yet know. They stick needles into our skin and pump liquids into our veins that dull our minds and dizzy our spirits and swell our tongues and fatten our limbs and torsos with tumorous layers. We are made stupid and isolated. Scattered, sinking islands in a sea of pus and excrement.

They have no faces behind their masks, but I can see through them, and I know what they do here.

Some of us are guiltier than others. We pad the hours with discussions, filling the gaps with possible reasons for our imprisonment. We comb through the transgressions in our pasts, weighing the gravity of our actions against the lengths of each of our stays. Some believe it to be retribution for crimes they thought to be wiped away by time or anonymity. Others grow mad, digging into their centers to find any crumb of misdeeds that could merit their situation. Some, whether their piety is valid or not, have decided that our hell has been brought on through no fault of their own, but that it is a collective revenge upon us for the worst crimes of the few truly evil among us. They have decided these walls are to contain a cleansing of our kind, to start anew.

For this reason, religions have sprouted, and groups have splintered into varying layers of insanity and faith. Some have called this the end of times. The masked creatures are angels of The Cleanse, here to issue forth the coming steps towards a bright utopia where only the purest of the imprisoned will emerge hand-in-hand with their captors to enjoy the fruits of our misery. They beg and plead when the masked creatures approach to drag them away through the metal curtains, screaming for forgiveness, crying for another day to prove their worth to the new world.

But each time they are taken, while others grovel and pray and celebrate as the massive machines whir, and the death-howls and pleasure-howls twist and converge until pleasure blankets the pain, and the death-howls become silence. The others celebrate this, because, with each new body cleansed by the masked creatures and hidden machines, that can only mean we are that much closer to the opened gates.

To some, the deaths of the others are the finest gifts given to those who witness. They love their captors. They love them and their masks and their machines. They love the cold walls and the injections, the starvation. They love it all. It is all a beautiful test to weed out the unworthy. And so, they prostrate themselves and submit and hurl words of admiration and thanks to the masked creatures as they defile us, squirming and fighting to catch a glimpse of the faces behind the masks as they pass. But I know it's all in vain. I know there are no eyes behind the masks. They harbor no soul, and so there are no windows to see what isn't there. I know this. I know what they do here.

Infighting has broken out between religious sects. What started as squabbles over the correctness of splintering theories quickly devolved into violent skirmishes, bloodied by the stubbornness of fervent beliefs. The creatures allow these brawls to continue to a point, only coming in to break up the onslaught once enough blood has been spilled. They will not allow a kill to occur if it's by our own hand. That is a right only they—and they alone—hold. They are the arbiters and the death dealers. We have no right to life, nor to end one.

Some of us claim to understand this practice, and so honor it. The Cleanse is not ours to make use of or accelerate. The

Cleanse is not our claim. It is solely the project and property of the masked creatures. To interfere would be to defy the holy process towards cultivating a new paradise. To some, this would be the vilest of sins. Their sect watches the others destroy themselves in the name of their beliefs, and shake their heads with pity, decidedly enlightened and above the masses of shortsighted heretics. To be so confident in one's understanding of our prison must be a comfort like nothing else available here.

One group tried to gain insight through more tangible means. There were five of them. They collected five discarded syringes off the cement floors. Four were still filled with pus and blood, but the syringes themselves were intact. One's syringe had been broken and bent after failing to pierce the skin of a subject. They then took the five syringes, burrowed them each deep inside one of the bales of hay that served as a bed, and, one by one, they took turns digging through the hay bale to find one hidden syringe. The unlucky fellow who found the broken syringe would be the one chosen for the operation.

Here, we have no names. We have no numbers. Nothing to signify or differentiate us outside of the appearances we were born with. In the minds of the masked creatures, we are equally qualified for slaughter. Any lines in the sand were drawn by our own kind. The one chosen was young. He was missing an ear. The oldest of the group, in a fit of guilt, volunteered in his place, but the decision was final. This group was adamant that no single life was worth saving over another. And so, this child was to go forward, and he accepted this fact with silence.

The plan was this: The child was to start a fight. It didn't matter with whom. He would continue to bludgeon and bite and thrash until he or his victim was near death. The masked creatures would then enter, as they always did, to stop the violence from reaching its climax. The child would then attack the masked creatures, spilling adrenaline into the bloodlust invited upon his captors. If all went as planned, the creatures would take the child away, dragging him through the metal curtain to meet his fate. That is when the second phase would occur.

I watched it happen.

Sick and dizzy from my daily injection, I heard a shrill gasp and looked out into the crowd of bodies. My vision was blurred and twisted behind a veil of side effects, but the first splatter of blood lit up the room like a strand of brilliant color inside a black-and-white photograph. My senses came alive and realigned to conjoin what I heard and saw. The crowd had parted and formed a wide circle like a cage for the two combatants. The child was tearing the skin off the other's face, his eyes pockets of fire as he screamed. Blood coated the floor and each other's bodies like war paint. It was beautiful and terrifying, and I wished for it to never end. My excitement and horror dulled the stupefying effects of the drugs. For a moment, I remembered that I was alive.

It wasn't until the other was nothing but a mangled pile of blood and pulp that the masked creatures appeared with weapons. Trampling through the ocean of sweating bodies, they brought the cries of our kind as they electrocuted all those in their path with their glowing rods. Crowd-controllers, we call them.

Through the open corridor the creatures made, I could see the body lying there, twitching and convulsing with labored breaths, and standing over him was the child, a river of blood running from his mouth. There was no anger in his eyes. The fires burned with intense fear, as if he'd been possessed and had just emerged from the trance to witness what he'd committed.

The rods struck him until his body submitted and collapsed, but, as the masked creatures reached in to pull the child away from the other, he leapt, knocking the creature closest to the ground.

I didn't want to save him. I just wanted to hurt something. I needed this feeling to never dissipate.

Before my mind became aware of what my body was doing, I was upon the creature. The taste of warm copper entered my mouth, and I saw beneath me the burrowed hole in the center of its stomach. I gnashed at the intestines that writhed like a cluster of worms underneath a rock, and the vibrant, wonderful bolts of electricity struck my back.

I was alive.

The prison erupted into chaos, the sound like explosives piercing my eardrums. Others joined in, toppling onto the masked creatures. Some were trying to take the rods from their hands. We outnumbered them. We were killing them, I knew, but I couldn't look away from the wound I'd created. I couldn't focus on anything but the shrill noise the masked creature was emitting: a death-howl. I'd never heard that sound from them before. It was more beautiful than anything I'd experienced. I wanted its mask. I wanted to rip the mask from its face and swallow its skin like the child did to one of our own.

The electric rods soon stopped striking my back, and the death-howls of the masked creatures multiplied around me as if I'd triggered the first in a series of ignitions. A gurgling came from underneath my victim's mask, and I knew it was choking on its own blood. I relinquished my jaw's grip on its innards and reached out to reveal its face—when a force struck me in the ribs, knocking me off the creature. I turned and saw the oldest of the group that had enacted the revolution.

"What have you done?" he shouted. *"You've ruined it all. You ruined our chance. We were going to get him out. We were going to take him back, and finally know what lies beyond the curtain. Now we're all going to die—all of us. You've doomed us."*

Masked creatures poured through every door, their rods creating waves of panic and pain that opened a path towards us. Rows of our zealots collapsed in reverence, praying and begging for forgiveness as the creatures approached.

"There's nothing to see beyond the curtain," I shouted back. "There is no utopia. There is no opening the doors. There is no freedom. I know what they do here. I just want to see their faces as they do it." I turned away in disgust and reached out to tear off the mask when the weight of an army fell upon me.

The rods struck every part of my flesh, until my skin was a blanket of fire, and consciousness failed me.

Between fading moments, I saw the child limp, dragged away, and the old man disappearing into the crowd of failed violence. The ground slid beneath me as my body was lurched forward, and the death-howls dissolved into a sea of familiar, percussive control.

I hoped I had killed the creature. My only regret was that I would never know if my face was the one it would remember in those final moments of agony.

I wanted to be its angel of the Cleanse.

I awoke to the sound of machinery. I lay on my back, and, as my eyes adjusted, I bore witness to a sight I never thought real.

There were few of us—a paltry few amongst the oldest of our kind—who weren't born here but were brought in as children from the outside world. Some spoke of it freely in a desperate attempt at dissociation, while others spoke of it little and in hushed tones to those they trusted. But all it took was one story from the outside-born for the tale to spread and take on its own life as folk legend.

It was a story often told to the dying or those broken by the abuse, to maintain hope or solace. It was the genesis of many great things and saved many from thrusting themselves into the arms of the masked creatures for volunteered execution. But it also brought out the ideologues, hungry for any sliver of control, twisting its purpose into stories of masked saviors and redemption and the coming utopia.

The story splintered into many interpretations, each molded in an image to suit whatever philosophy any of us chose to cling to. The stories that formed became like currency to be hoarded, because they bred hope in the minds of those who believed. But one currency had to be universal—otherwise who was to say which system was correct? Thus, contempt was sowed into the population and violence arose. Bodies could pile, as they did every day, but hope—hope was necessary. And its source had to be undoubtedly true for it to maintain its effect.

The original tale became so mutated that no one quite remembers how it went. All those who first told it are now gone, whether from starvation, suicide, murder, or they simply found themselves on the other side of the metal curtain, as we all will one day. That's why I only took credence in one truth: The masked creatures come for us all. Anything else is inconsequential—words and ideas to fill the space between the present moment and the inevitable finale.

But what every mutation had in common—the single facet of the story that had never changed—was what I was looking up at in that moment: The sky. A bright blue sky. With fluffy, white clouds and a big, round, yellow sun. A world without a ceiling.

I lifted myself onto my haunches and felt sticky, warm liquid coating my back. A pool of blood surrounded me. Believing it to be my own, I jerked upright and twisted around to get a look at my wounds yet only found singed ovals of cauterized flesh left by crowd-controllers. That's when I saw the child beside me.

He was still unconscious, eyes fluttering, his life filtered through shallow breaths, but his body was mutilated. If it weren't for the missing ear, I wouldn't have been able to tell him apart from any other wounded animal. His opponent inflicted the marks and abrasions—I'd never known the masked creatures to damage us to this extent. Their methods of violence were invasive and mental, never superficial. Why this was, none of us knew.

The sun's glare was hot and blinding and alien, but I could see we were contained within a gated pen. Beyond the gate was something massive and mechanical, and it was so loud that I couldn't hear my words as I shook the child and spoke: "Hey. Hey, stay here. I'm here. Wake up. Open your eyes."

The child stirred and gave a grunt that vibrated through his broken ribs into my palm.

"Keep your eyes open. Focus on me."

"Did it work?" asked the child.

I glanced around the room outside the pen. Dozens of large objects swayed in the air, strung up by metal wires. I couldn't make out what they were. I had little understanding of the outside world—if any—but my instincts were at odds with what I was looking at. Something wasn't right.

"Did I make it? Is this it? *Utopia*?" The child's eyes darted across the heavens of his new surroundings, his neck seemingly unable to move. "It's beautiful."

With a jolt, the machinery stopped. From the silence came an arrhythmic symphony of droplets hitting the floor, like a hundred leaking faucets.

"Rain?" said the child. "It's *real*."

I followed the metal wires down from the sky, allowing my double vision to refocus on the objects they suspended.

That was the moment I saw. My lungs paralyzed, I stared. I stared until I was sure.

My mind needed time to wrap itself around the image, but I saw, and I knew, and I understood at once.

"It's not rain," I said. "Don't try to get up. Don't say another word. Keep your eyes open and don't look anywhere but ahead."

A droplet landed on my shoulder.

Warm. Sticky. Crimson droplet.

Fear trembled the child's voice: "W—What's going on?"

"*Do as I say*," I hissed.

I counted thirty of them. Hanging upside-down, slashed across the throat. Arranged in rows like ornaments. Blood seeping out, dripping onto the killing room floor. Thirty of us.

This revelation led to the next. In the face of horror, my mind was able to see the world equally for what it was: Artifice.

The wires hung not from the sky, but from a painted ceiling, a bastardized caricature of the outside realm we clung to for generations—a bastardization of hope itself.

Looming over us like an alien monolith, like only that which could have birthed the angels of the Cleanse, was the massive machine: The Archangel of Death. It was the conductor that orchestrated the score for our prison—the all-consuming and forever-enduring death-howls.

"We've crossed the metal curtain," I said.

"Good," the child replied. "That's good. Then the others will come for us, and you can tell them everything you see. They'll come for us soon. They told me they would."

With the machine asleep, the child's words echoed off the killing room's walls.

Paranoia overcame my heartbeat, and I felt the weight of invisible eyes upon us as I pressed my face against the child's ear: "*Quiet.*"

Heavy footsteps approached from a tall set of stairs above the machine. Masked creatures made their way down the narrow walkway and formed pairs underneath two of the hanging bodies. Each pair pulled bodies off their hooks, one taking the burden upon its shoulder as its partner held the dangling head from behind, ignoring the blood cascading down its back.

The child and I stared as the small crew climbed another walkway to the belly of the machine. There were glances exchanged between predator and prey, savior and sinner, but no words were shared, and they continued with the task at hand.

A button was pressed in the small, caged terminal that served as a control room for the machine, and the massive conveyer belt extending like a demon's tongue screeched and chugged. At the end of the conveyer belt was a large receptacle with steel teeth that gnashed in intervals.

The child froze with fear, his eyes glued to the painted sun, his breaths shallower and shallower as the drops fell and joined the growing pool beneath his wounds like rain in the ocean.

The creatures dropped each body onto the conveyer belt, and all of us watched the dead float towards the gnashing teeth. It was like watching souls condemned to the deepest ring of Hell.

And that's what it was. That's what it had to be. This was the afterlife all had received before us. This was the utopia the zealots had proclaimed: the fangs at the mouth of the beast.

Behold its majesty.

The bodies fell and disappeared into a pink mist that rose from the receptacle like a winter fog. The machine sputtered, and, from its jagged maw, came the terrible grinding of bone and flesh. At the base of the receptacle was a spigot with an open-faced barrel waiting beneath. Out of the spigot came a thick, pink mixture filling up the barrel. The spigot dripped three times before coughing out mist. One of the creatures pressed a button, and the machine returned to its slumber.

It was as if they'd tamed a demon, leashed a wild animal, and subdued it with the sacrifice of our kind. I had borne witness to a ritual never meant to be seen, the religion of a foreign species, the religion that our prison was built for and upon; the true faith that served as the nucleus of our existence, hidden behind the metal curtain.

I'd stepped through the tangible veil of our afterlife, and laid eyes upon the answer we'd sought after—the source of our eternal question. I'd seen the only higher power that mattered.

In horror, I was enlightened.

Our Hell was their Utopia. A truth preserved in the greatest lie.

I'd found God, and I was going to kill It.

The creatures turned their sights to us and began walking towards the pen, forming a wide half-circle, creeping like hunters approaching two fawns. One of the creatures stopped before the locked gate to our cage, reaching to open the door to our demise, when the sound of something wonderful erupted behind the metal curtain: Violence. Chaos and shrill violence.

The creatures whipped their heads and froze, listening to the unmistakable noise. They were unarmed. The smell of fear seeped out from behind their masks. The sound grew louder, wider, heavier, more forceful. Something was coming.

The child tried to speak, only able to release a choking gurgle as blood spilled from his tongue, but he smiled.

The foundation was crumbling.

Then, like leaks in a dam giving way to a torrent of floodwater, they entered—a handful, then dozens, then hundreds. Bleeding and bruised and coated with fluids not their own. They poured into their afterlife as one massive organism, and in that first moment of recognition, a silence bloomed, so thick, it pulled the oxygen out of the room.

From within the mob of our kind, appearing from the nucleus of the revolution, came the familiar old man. Dragging behind him was the dead body of a masked creature. Like a vanquished combatant presented to an enemy officer, he thrust the body at the feet of the stunned captors, and it lay there stiff, shortening the empty space between the two sides.

Just as the tension seemed to burst into further violence, a voice from the mob screamed out: "*Look! Look at the sky! It's true! It's all true!*"

"*The bodies!*" came another, and the eyes of the crowd all looked away from the heavens to witness the reality. I waited for the moment of recognition, for the believers to collapse into anger and horror and retribution.

But instead, came the voice of a third: "*They're bringing us closer to the sky! A rebirth into the new world! Look! Look there! The mouth of the giant! The entrance to Utopia! Quickly, everyone! We've arrived at the door! We don't have to wait any longer!*"

Like a multi-headed animal, the crowd gazed upon the machine and its jagged-toothed receptacle. The zealots moved to the front, gingerly stepping closer to the masked creatures still frozen and silenced by survival instinct.

"*Thank you!*" one shouted, prostrating himself before the creatures. "*I never doubted for a second! I always believed! I beg you, saviors, allow us entry—together, hand-in-hand! Have we not served you well? Have we not listened and obeyed?*"

I was stunned. I'd seen the truth, and I knew what they did here. I could have screamed out, proclaimed the true purpose of their gods, denied the false prophets with proof.

But I didn't.

I wanted them to discover the truth.

The child's eyes grew mad, darting back and forth, trying to pierce into me, to be his voice, to say what we both understood. But all that came out was a garbled pool of blood and vomit, his limbs twitching and body convulsing in a final, failed attempt to conjure the last of his strength and stand.

Ignoring the zealots, the old man heard the wet sounds emitted, and turned to our pen. In a single moment, he'd charged into the gate, bashing with the full force of his body, severing the lock. He flew forward as the gate crashed onto the ground.

He leaned over the child, panic thickening his blood, and, before he could speak, I whispered so only he and the child could hear: "Stay," I said. "Let it happen. Let them have their Utopia."

The old man stared at me in horror. He was disgusted. I realized then that I wasn't the only one who knew.

If he was going to respond, it was stifled by a final outburst from somewhere in the mob, the last needed for the event to proceed: "They're murderers! Use your eyes! See what they've done! An eye for an eye! AN EYE FOR AN EYE!"

What fascinated me most about what happened next, was that it wasn't the words that caused the mob to charge, but that words caused one of the creatures to flee. That's when it happened. It was a predatory instinct to kill. Not the words or ideas espoused, but the simple act of retreat. The wolves saw the rabbit run. That's all it came down to. That's all any of it ever was. Instinct.

The moment the creature had turned, the mob came alive with bloodlust and its three companions were buried beneath a pile of writhing flesh and flailing limbs. Splinters of the mob took chase after the massacred creatures' companion and stopped short as it swung closed the gate to the control room and locked itself inside. There were screams and clangs and spit and fury, and the creature stood pressed into the corner, cowering over the panel of buttons that gave their god life.

A group of zealots clawed their way up the stairs, trying to push the others from the gate, shouting, "Leave it! Leave it be! It saved us all! They built for us the path out! The way is open—go now! Into the mouth of God!"

The words shook sects of the war party from their vicious fugue state, and, like insects towards a light in the dark, they disregarded the creature without another look and leapt onto the conveyer belt.

The old man held the dying child's head in his arms and looked up at me. "You have to do something. Put an end to this, there's another way—there has to be."

I watched the swarm converge upon the mouth of the beast, and the creature's hand trembling above the button. "They deserve to know," I said. "They deserve to know what they do here. We all deserve it."

Still, more of our kind crashed against the gate like waves against the beach, desperate to tear into the creature before meeting their Utopia. Retribution had to come first.

"You're as evil as them," the old man spat.

The mob was breaking away to join the others on the beast's tongue, leaving behind piles of meat and blood that were once their captors.

"As who?" I answered.

Bodies began to drop into the mouth, collapsing on top of one another. It was a mad dash towards salvation, each individual a piece of a perfectly encapsulated entity spiting the last to reach the same exact goal. They scratched and pulled and shoved and bit and screeched to find a glimpse of beyond, of beneath, and so they tumbled down the throat together in clumps like tumors, until the mouth was full.

And the god came alive.

The surviving creature had found the moment and pressed the button. The conveyer belt chugged and clicked, and the metal teeth whirred, gnashing, gnashing gnashing, and the pile of sinners lurched as those at the bottom were swallowed and digested.

Pink mist sprayed up through the fissures of the great mass, dousing the floor and painted sky. There were cries of horror and of prayer, and there was pain, but it was smothered as a specter for the next layer in line to believe or dismiss.

Still, the bodies approached and fell, adding weight and stress to the beast that had gotten its fill, that wanted no more sacrifice, but it was created for this purpose, and it was all it knew, and so it continued to tear bone and flesh as it coughed in bloated agony.

Smoke rose from the machine's armor-skin, and the miasma of charred meat and scalding oil tinged my nostrils. The conveyer belt halted as if colliding with a wall, and the cries and prayer were muted by an insurmountable eruption.

The Gates of Hell tore open.

The force of the explosion hit me before the flames, lifting me off my feet as if spirited away after death. But then came the heat, the molten plasma singeing my skin, bringing my mind back to full awareness. My ears rang, and my vision trembled like my eyes had been shaken within their sockets by an invisible entity.

As the ringing faded, I waited for screams to pierce the veil of static but all that remained was silence. Silence, and a sensation I'd never felt. It cooled my burnt flesh like the ectoplasm of ghosts passing through me, gently kissing at the wounds.

The dust settled, and my vision found its footing. There, looming over my prone body was the hollowed corpse of God. The great machine was a skeleton of its former self, orange pockets of flames licking the air from a wide-open hole in the center of its anatomy. The control room had collapsed in on itself, burying the last creature in its final moment of autonomy. Smoldering fires spit from its gnarled gate; the brain severed. Fragments of limbs and jawbones and teeth and tongues and fingers lay strewn across the cement floor, each scattered piece of sinner and savior made indistinguishable from one another.

To my side were the old man and the child, the eldest huddled over the other, together breathing heavy sighs, their eyes squeezed shut. Again, came the unfamiliar sensation, like a beckoning call, and I looked out towards the echoing voice it carried.

And there, where once stood an impenetrable wall, the limits of our prison, of their temple, was a puncture wound. What lay beyond was no mirage, no artificial farce.

An exit.

"Get up," I said, shaking the old man. "Get on your feet and look."

They both stirred, opening their eyes to look upon me before experiencing the same foreign call from the other side, and they saw.

The three of us stood, leaning upon one another, the child wilting, rivulets of blood draining from his lips, each of us unable to speak, unable to put words to what presented itself through the prison's killing wound.

As we approached, the cold air wrapping around us like a cloak, the old man finally whispered: "It's nothing like what I remember."

These were the last words I heard him speak, though the wet gleam in his eyes reflected memories never shared and would never again be relived. That, perhaps, is exactly why they had been laid to rest with the last of his generation. He knew.

Framed by the crumbling exterior, like a portrait of the artist's nightmare, was the world.

No sun. No blue sky. No rain. No grass.

They dotted the flat, gray surface like hundreds of anthills in a desert, blanketed by a black wall of smog. Suffocating the landscape like a multiplying virus, swallowing any iota of beauty that may have once existed—that only existed within the mind of a single old man.

Identical in every way, in each possible facet of order and the mundane. Leaving only enough space for cement pathways to snake through like dried riverbeds.

Prisons.

Hundreds and hundreds.

And hundreds.

Prisons.

Prisons.

Prisons.

What else could I do, but—

Laugh?

The Greatest Show On Earth

Her voices flickers between the walls, somewhere out of reach, echoing off the wide, curved confines of the amphitheater. It comes in waves, the words lost behind the static of the chattering crowd like the apocalyptic hum of an approaching locust horde. Their conversations pirouette into one great noise devoid of any particular purpose, but the volume ebbs and flows, bouncing off each other's empty responses. They are excited. We are anticipating something fantastic to appear upon the bare, backlit stage.

I didn't buy a ticket, nor was I informed of the evening's entertainment. I floated to this place like a spirit haunting the room, unable to leave or enter, but always existing as an ethereal body, ignored by the congregation. They are far too enamored by what's to come to pay attention to those around them, only letting their words intertwine with no goal but to voice their quarantined mind and collectively say the same thing to nobody at all: *I am here to celebrate.*

The phone in my hand twists around my fingers like a skittish mouse. I see her name next to the number, but I'm unable to coax the phone into submission so I can press the **call** button. The digits interchange and morph before my eyes, toying with me, forbidding me from committing them to memory. Somewhere in my mind is the correct order, but any recollection dissolves into a chasm before the image becomes vivid enough to discern.

Sometimes the overwhelming din of the crowd falls away when the black curtains rustle onstage, and, in that moment of hushed silence, her voice screams out, crashing against the walls like a provoked bull in a pen. The amphitheater trembles as if struck by an earthquake, but no one pulls their eyes away from the curtains. This is what they have ached and wished for their entire lives. Nothing will remove them from the revelation. Nothing else could possibly matter but what lies behind.

I do not know what awaits us. The only thing I know, the only thought my mind allows to appear in detail, is that what lies behind the curtain is the thing I most do not want to witness. Anything else could appear on the stage, and the terror strangling me would release its grip, but, at the very base of my being, I know that any of these things are not what is to come. It is the terrifying certainty of this event. It is unavoidable. It is exactly what these people have come to see.

When I try to lock eyes with fellow audience members, their faces contort and twist like seawater at the whim of a hurricane. What remain constant are the black pockets where eyes would be, and—though I can't see life inside the abysses that seem to go for miles through the backs of their heads—I feel the intention and focus somewhere deep within that tells me their awareness is palpably upon me, if only for a moment, before turning their attention back to the stage.

There is nothing to do but wait for the main event.

The warning is given when the massive crystalline chandeliers dim, and nothing remains but the red floodlights illuminating the center stage. The crowd falls silent, a kind of silence I've never experienced before. I can hear the blood moving through my veins, buzzing, my heart leaping inside my chest like a trapped creature violently trying to escape from a cardboard box. This will be the greatest show on Earth.

A man walks onto the center stage. He wears an extravagant red tuxedo, the color accentuated beneath the floodlights' glow, its coattails draping far behind him upon the floor like a slug's mucus trail. A black top hat sits on his head, adding a foot to his squat stature. His mustache is thick and manicured to curl at the ends like a carnival barker from an era long passed. His face does not contort when I watch. Despite his appearance that feels alien, he is the only real and life-like entity I've seen here. But something about him unsettles me more than the melting faces of my peers.

There is no humanity in his presentation, in his eyes. His face stabs me at the bottom of my stomach with the same, distant feeling one gets as a child separated from a parent in a grocery store. He is the loneliest man I have ever seen, but that isolation doesn't come from within himself, it emanates out towards the crowd in tangible waves. He feels none of it but creates it for others to absorb. He is the acidic, tainted water filling the lungs of a man drowning in the ocean.

The anticipatory silence of the crowd is shattered when the phone in my hand erupts with a harsh ringing, intensified by the amphitheater's acoustics.

All at once, the fluid jigsaw faces of every person turn to me like a hive of predators that have caught the scent of blood. The man on stage, once grinning, zeroes in on the disturbance and his face becomes fierce and stone-like. His eyes, directed upon me, physically hurt, as if his gaze has released a poison that seeps beneath my skin like radioactive fallout and sets every nerve ending in my body on fire.

But the distraction is worth the agony, for when I look down upon the screen, I see her name, illuminated and bold, unchanging and clearly legible.

The audience collapses upon me as I try to accept the call. Before I can make contact, a faceless man snatches the phone.

He throws it onto the ground, shattering it with the stomp of his boot. He holds a finger up to his lips that swirl around his face like water circling a drain. *Shhh*, he says. *Shhh*.

Again, from somewhere beyond us, her voice screams in horror, filling up the empty space of the amphitheater. The chandeliers sway and crash against each other like wind chimes in a storm. As though this is the cue the man on stage is waiting for, the toothy grin reappears across his face.

He holds out a rigid arm with his palm out, offering up the main event. Without a word, he then walks off stage, the coattails last to disappear, following behind like a loyal pet.

The crowd's attention falls away from me and my *faux pas*, and each black hole is directed back toward the curtains.

Before I can see what's been revealed as the curtains pull away, the spectators leap to their feet, screaming and cheering, their outstretched arms blocking my view.

I wrestle my way between two men in front of me to catch a glimpse of what's caused this explosive reaction. What I see is something I cannot make sense of.

A young woman wearing nothing but tattered, brown rags and a pained grimace stands at the center. The red floodlights aim directly over her, creating a glowing circle like a ring of fire that gives the appearance of an inescapable prison cell. The audience's ovation is deafening, building until the claps cause my ears to ring. This moment they've waited for has lived up to their expectations and more. They've entered a place of ecstasy, as if any life remaining within this woman is being sapped and absorbed by her onlookers with each passing second of applause, and, beneath its weight, her legs give out and she crumples onto her knees. She opens her mouth to scream, or to cry, but she is silenced by the thunderous response of the crowd.

This goes on until the woman begins to hack and cough as if something is caught in her throat, and the applause stops flat. The unwavering attention of ten-thousand black holes falls upon her, and the air becomes thick with static energy. Their twisting bodies all lean in closer, anxious to bear witness to every detail of what is next to come.

The woman's eyes bulge, and her mouth gapes, and her tongue hangs over her scabbed bottom lip, and a torrent of black liquid ejects from her body, pooling upon the stage. The stench burns when inhaled, and the whole of the amphitheater fills with the miasma emitted from the substance. It is unavoidable. The crowd responds with a chorus of *Ohhhh*s and reserved claps from pockets of the room.

Something inside me twinges with the acute urge to leap onto the stage and help this woman, but I can't bring myself to do it. I am trapped in place, watching it all unfold, paralyzed by fear or disgust or awe.

She struggles to stand, her body trembling, and again parts of the audience clap while some moan as if watching a matador narrowly escape the bull's horns. Like a matador's audience, they've come to see what happens when it all goes wrong. They want destruction. They want the worst-case scenario. We are ancient Romans in the Coliseum, holding our breath until the lone gladiator fails in combat.

The woman wipes the oil-like bile from her chin and stumbles backwards, and her eyes grow wide. Something new is happening. She holds her hands in front of her face, staring at them as if learning that they're attached to her body. Before the audience can gauge what's occurring, she opens her mouth again to release a silent scream. Deep wrinkles and spots appear on her skin, and her fingers gnarl like the limbs of a diseased tree. Dark bags form beneath her eyes, and black veins protrude, running down her legs and neck like polluted rivers. Her spine contorts, forcing her into a submissive, hunched posture.

The long, brown hair draping her shoulders thins and falls onto the stage in clumps. The color in what's left of the patches upon her head drains away and turns a sickly gray. She falls back onto her side, and the *crack* of a bone breaking reverberates off the walls. Her body seems to shrink, and she curls into the fetal position, the blood-red lights burning through her skin so as to make her appear translucent. Ghost-like. A shadow of what existed only seconds before.

The audience erupts with triumphant shouts. There is no reverence in their acclaim. It's bloodlust. They want more. *Keep going. Go further. Don't stop. This is what we are owed.*

She continues to wither like a fruit picked from the tree and left to rot beneath the sun, curling her knees into her chest, taking on the form of an aborted fetus tossed upon the hospital floor, until the only sign of life that remains are her eyes, still open, vividly aware of what's happening to the vessel they reside within. As her body shrinks, her eyes seem to grow by contrast, and they are wet, and they glimmer in the light, and they speak in silence, louder than the boisterous approval of the crowd. They say, *Help me. Help me. Help me. I'm still here. Help me.*

The man in the top hat returns to the stage, and the audience's elation multiplies tenfold. Every faceless creature leaps onto their feet, compelled to shout and holler and clap and clap and clap. Their applause is like warfare. The amphitheater shakes, and the chandeliers crash, and the floodlights flash until I can see nothing but white splotches like fireworks.

Somewhere beyond the chaos, a faint noise floats just beneath. It is constant, and, though its volume is nothing to that of the clamor of the audience, it pierces through and remains. It stings. It burns. It hurts so much that it brings my vision back to focus, and I see the man standing over the dying woman, grinning, holding his arms out towards her, not to help, but to present the intended results of the show. The finale.

Look at what I've done for you.

As the man takes a bow, and the woman cowers and convulses, devolving into a limp pile of flesh, and the spectators' applause becomes like the seven trumpets of Revelation, otherworldly and impossible to ignore, this other sound, this separate and familiar sound, grows louder and louder until it centers inside my ears for only me to listen. And suddenly, the cacophony of the amphitheater disappears, and I understand the source of the noise.

They say when your ears ring, you're hearing cells dying. They say you will never hear that exact frequency ever again. It is something to remember. That's the only way that it will continue to exist.

Months have passed since my mother's flatlining heart monitor awoke me on the chair beside her hospital bed. Months have passed since I deleted the voice messages that tethered me, however weakly, to her ghost. But the dream never leaves. Every night, the man returns, and the faceless audience, and the decaying woman, and the unanswerable calls, and her shrieking voice, and the long, painful, sobering, buzzing sound that brought me back to my waking life only for me to miss—by mere seconds—the conclusion of her own.

The dream never leaves because the sound, the shrill ringing, is committed to memory, and that sound will never end until it, too, one day beckons me to the amphitheater as the star of the show.

Maybe then, when the man takes a bow over my dying body, and the applause drowns out my terror of the coming unknown, the sound will cease.

But until that inevitable time, each night, I visit her.

In the only way my mind can ever allow it again.

I will take what I can.

A Ticket For The Night Bus

Maxwell stood alone at the abandoned bus stop. Wind blew across the thin fabric of his hospital gown, raising goose bumps along his exposed skin. Across the empty street, the old church sat in shadows, and the bell atop its steeple rang out, echoing into the night. Twelve times, the bell rang, and Maxwell listened, the lingering space between each reverberating chime was like a fermata written on a living sheet of music.

The church too appeared abandoned but, somewhere within, someone kept its weak pulse alive, creating music amidst midnight's silence. A monotone note that repeated, bounding off crumbling and graffitied walls, until the final sound floated away, beyond where Maxwell could see.

As if the renewed quiet were an invitation, two lights appeared from down the street, dissolving the surrounding darkness as the chugging, hulking vehicle drew closer. The bus stopped in front of Maxwell, and the door swung open. The driver didn't speak, nor remove his hands from the vibrating wheel, nor take his eyes off the road ahead.

Maxwell stepped onto the bus without a word. The door closed behind him. Before he could find a seat, the bus began to drive. In the rearview mirror, the old church disappeared behind a black veil. All that remained was what existed inside the bus, and the headlights' yellow beams eating away at the shadows like maggots on a corpse.

Three people sat on either side of the aisle, each taking up a row of seats. Closest to the front was a tall, dark-haired, severe-looking man. He wore a tailored, black three-piece suit that helped distract from the skeletal melancholy of his face. He was handsome in the way a drug addict can be: with a pale, defined jawline and eyes sunken deep into their sockets like they hadn't slept in days. No gestures or words were exchanged as Maxwell walked past.

Behind the gaunt man, sitting in the opposite row, was a young woman, fidgeting and rosy-cheeked as if she'd just finished a strenuous run. Where the first man appeared overdressed, she presented the opposite: Nothing but two towels were wrapped around her, one covering her body and the other carefully knotted around her head. The towels were still wet; a small puddle of water had formed around her feet. When Maxwell walked by, she shot her arm up towards him and sharply inhaled as if about to speak, before straightening back into her clenched posture, then turned to look out the window into the abyss.

Sitting at the back of the bus and staring directly at Maxwell, was a child. She was in pajamas. They were decorated with little pink and purple elephants. Her arms were wrapped around a stuffed rabbit. Its ears were floppy and hung past its feet. The rabbit looked as if it was once white but now dirtied and loved until its fur had turned brown. She squeezed the rabbit tight, holding it to her face like a lifebuoy keeping her from sinking into an ocean only she could see.

Maxwell took a seat in the row just ahead of the child and looked out the window into the darkness.

After a few moments of silence, gentle footsteps approached from behind, and shallow, raggedy breaths began tickling the back of his neck. "This is Franklin. Franklin says hi."

Maxwell turned and shoved in front of his face was the rabbit, held by two little hands underneath its arms.

When he failed to respond, the child spoke again: "He's my ticket. So, you can't hold him. I'm not supposed to let him go yet. He says hi though."

Maxwell looked around the bus, hoping for one of the passengers to corral the child. The man continued facing forward, but the woman watched, her eyes piercing and wide as if trying to communicate, her right fist clenched and trembling upon her bouncing knee.

"Where's yours?" the child asked. "Do you have a ticket?"

Before he could answer, an authoritative voice came from the front of the bus: "Leave him be. Sit down."

The child's eyes fixated on the space over Maxwell's shoulder like a deer hearing a gunshot, and she bolted back to her seat.

The man twisted around to face the two, and his gaze shifted between Maxwell and the scorned child. "That's none of your business," he said. "I'm sure your parents taught you better."

Though the man was reprimanding the child, Maxwell felt as if he were speaking to the both of them. A thick layer of guilt seeped into his body, prickling the skin like his limbs had fallen asleep.

"If he wants to show you, he will."

The child tucked her knees into her chest and squeezed the rabbit again, burying her face into its matted fur.

Maxwell waited for the man to stop glaring and face forward before getting the child's attention with a subtle hand gesture.

She looked up, the rabbit still concealing half of her face, her eyes glazed and red with tears.

Hi, Franklin, he mouthed, and waved at the stuffed animal, forcing a closed smile.

The child pinched the rabbit's limb between her fingers and wagged it back and forth. "He's not very nice," she whispered, her eyes darting towards the man's head. "I don't like him."

"Me neither," Maxwell whispered back. "I bet he's just grumpy he doesn't have his own rabbit like Franklin."

She giggled into the stuffed animal's floppy ears. "Yeah. I bet that's it."

Maxwell began to turn when the child tapped his shoulder. "*Psst.*"

Just outside of view, he could feel the woman's gaze burning into the side of his head, communicating as clearly as if she were screaming out loud, aching for him to acknowledge her.

"*Psst,*" the child tried again.

"What is it?"

"Why are you wearing that funny dress?"

"It's not a dress. They give it to you when you go where I went."

"Where did you go?"

Maxwell opened his mouth and, as the first word was about to escape, he realized the memory wasn't there. He didn't have an answer. He swore he knew—only a moment before, he knew—but it was gone. There was nothing. "I'm not sure," he said.

"Oh. That's okay. You'll remember soon. Once we get closer."

Maxwell paused. "You think so?"

"Yep. I know so. All the fuzzy stuff from before—it'll start going back into your head soon. The bus does that. But you have to wait and be quiet."

"How do you know that?"

"'Cause. I know lots of things I didn't used to. Franklin didn't used to be Franklin. He was just Bunny Rabbit. But the road started to get darker, and all the stuff outside the window went away. And then I remembered his name is Franklin. So, I bet you'll remember where you got your dress. Just as long as you remembered your ticket."

Maxwell stared into the child's eyes for a long time. Waiting until he could see through her.

But the child was there, staring back.

"Okay," he said. When he turned, there was the woman.

Her eyes danced back and forth between urgent glances at Maxwell and the corners of the bus, as if following ghosts amongst the shadows. She gestured with one hand beneath her knee, compelling Maxwell to come sit beside her.

He slid into the woman's row, his feet making a wet slap as they sank into the water spreading out from her dripping body.

"Is it coming back to you?" she asked, her gaze focused on the back of the bus driver's head.

Maxwell kept a watchful eye on the man in the row opposite and ahead of them as he spoke: "No, not yet."

"Do you have it on you?"

He looked down at his hospital gown and held out his palms. "Where would I keep it?"

"Well, you need to find it. You wouldn't have been let on here if you hadn't brought something."

In the rearview mirror, Maxwell could see the eyes reflected back, staring at him. Black eyes, obsidian eyes, cloaked in shadows but backlit by the sickly yellow headlights, dispelling the evidence of night like windshield wipers in the rain.

"What happens if I don't?"

"You will," she answered. "Because you have to. You don't have a choice. You got on the bus."

Maxwell looked at the woman, studying her face, her limbs, the wet knots of hair dangling from her shoulders, the water falling from the strands and landing on her pink skin like rain streaming over a cliff. As hard as he tried to focus, her features seemed to shift, refusing to settle in place, like a Rubik's cube rearranging itself before his eyes. "Do I know you?"

"Does it matter?" She opened the fist resting upon her knee, revealing a small diamond ring, as if the whole time she'd been clutching a lump of coal, squeezing until the pressure transformed it. "I can't lose this. It's all that's left before everything else leaves me. Just because you made it on the bus, doesn't mean it's over yet."

The sight of the ring burned somewhere within a hole in his mind. Where there was once a blank space, a fire had been lit, cleansing the debris of amnesia from one corner of the empty room that had enveloped him upon stepping foot inside the bus. "What is that?" he asked.

"It's an anchor. Find yours, before we reach our stop. That's all that matters." Her face was coming back into focus. Pieces of the past gluing themselves back together. Like flashes of light bursting through the canopy of trees while driving down a wooded street, glimpses shone into memories before fizzling away: a beach. A bed. A television screen. Laughter. An empty room. Silence. Wires. Machinery. And tears.

Constant throughout them all was the feeling of comfort—comfort that faded more and more with each glimpse, until all that remained was fear. The kind of fear you don't forget. And yet it was as if it were the first time he'd ever felt it. A troubling sense of *déjà vu* overtook him, and, without another word, Maxwell stood, walked up to the gaunt man, and sat down.

Refusing to look away from the front of the bus, the man spoke: "Enjoying the ride?"

"I need my ticket."

"Why do you think I have it?" The man turned to face Maxwell, his eyes pockets of blue ocean water.

"Because I don't know you."

"I don't know you either. I know about you, though. Not much. But some. If you'd just be patient, I'm sure it'll come to you."

"I'm running out of time."

The man opened his mouth and laughed. "Do you see a clock? Look outside."

The world surrounding the bus was a swirling vortex, like layers of fog blown to and fro in a pitch-black night. There was no longer a road beneath the wheels. The vehicle was propelling like a spaceship in the cosmos.

"We're all strangers here," the man continued. "You don't know the child. I don't know the child. You could ask her the same question, and she'd have the same answer. It's between you and the driver. But no one talks to the bus driver."

"I know," said Maxwell.

"Ah, see? It's coming back to you, bit by bit. Be patient. Enjoy the ride." He gestured behind him, towards the little girl kicking her feet and mumbling to the stuffed rabbit. "This will always be easier for those who don't question it. That much, I know. And that much, I can tell you."

"What else? What else can you tell me? Anything."

The man peered over his shoulder, at the woman staring into her trembling legs. "I can tell you that she's been here the longest. She was alone when I got on. Then the child arrived. Then you. Because of that, I'd imagine she knows more than me. So, I'm not the one to ask. But asking questions—that's my point. It's probably best not to. Do you want to see something?"

The man reached into his jacket and brandished a switchblade. Its handle was black and engraved with two initials. He pushed the button beneath the hilt and the silver, serrated blade popped out.

"This was my father's," the man said.

He twisted the knife around in his hand, and let it dangle from his fingers as he talked, eyeing it like it was a mouse he'd captured in the kitchen.

"He always had it on him. Every day. 'Always be ready,' he'd tell me. 'Always be prepared for the worst. You have to always be prepared for the worst, and when it happens—which it will—you can't act out of emotion. You have to react like you would with any mundane, day-to-day task. Accept that it's happening and do whatever you have to do—like...like you're taking out the trash.' That's how you keep going. You put your head down, and you put one foot in front of the other. Just like with anything else."

He folded the blade back but kept holding it, clutching it in his fist like the woman clutching the ring.

"My father always talked like that. When I was a kid, he seemed so wise. Like he knew everything there was to know. Like he was invincible with knowledge. But then he dropped dead of a heart attack. You can't prepare your way out of that. You can't outsmart a clogged artery. And now I'm older than he was when he died. I always held on to this thing to remind me that maybe I'd be as wise and prepared as my father. But just a little better. A little smarter. Yet here I am. I don't feel smarter. I don't feel prepared. In fact, I feel like an idiot. Wandering through life. Utterly clueless. And that used to bother me. But now, I've realized that he probably felt the same way. He just did what he knew despite it all: Head down, one foot in front of the other. Don't think about it. Just...act until the curtains draw."

Maxwell focused on the man's nose, studying the black pores dotting his sun-starved face, unable to look him in the eyes. "Why are you telling me this?"

"Because you seem like you could use this more than me." The man hesitated but handed the sheathed switchblade to Maxwell. "Just as a reminder. Whatever is going to happen, will happen. And when it does...act. Don't overthink it."

"But this is your ticket," said Maxwell. "It must be. I can't take this."

"Maybe," the man answered, turning to look out into oblivion. "Maybe not. We'll have to wait and see when we arrive."

"Where are we going?"

"I'm sure you already know that. Failing to accept what you already know won't do you any favors."

Maxwell fell silent.

He stood to leave, and the man talked into the window: "It feels like returning from the dead, doesn't it? All these memories pouring back in. Like someone finally remembered to pay the electricity bill. I can see again."

"Something about it," said Maxwell. "It doesn't feel right."

"Well, that's the thing: Once you're out of the dark, you may not like what you see. One foot in front of the other, though. Yeah? *Left-right-left-right.* There you are. *Left-right-left-right.* Go on then. And try to enjoy yourself. We'll be there soon."

Maxwell stepped into the aisle.

A hand gripped his arm as he passed. The woman looked up at him, digging her nails into his flesh, trying to pull him closer. Her whole body trembled, and a grimace pulled the skin taut against her clenched jaw. "I remember everything," she said. "I remember...everything. I'm fucking scared. Please help me."

Maxwell allowed her grip to guide him into the seat beside her. "There's nothing to be scared of," he lied, and slid his hand over hers. A moment of panic set in as he felt the fire burning away at more hidden memories when he looked into her face.

Reality was becoming fluid, melting away from the inside, but he brushed away these feelings. Pockets of time flashed behind his eyes, and he pushed the images down like stifling vomit. But what remained was the impressions those moments carved into the walls of his empty room. There was no place to escape. The bus became like a coffin, an echo chamber, forcing the poisonous residue down his throat, screaming at him to accept what he knew. Still, Maxwell fought back.

The woman held up the ring, the growing light of the ethereal cosmos seen through the window glinting off the diamond. "I never forgot about you," she said. "I did everything I could. I just hope you can forgive me."

"I don't understand, honey." Maxwell flinched as the word left his mouth.

Outside, thunderous booms erupted in the void, shaking the bus like a plane during turbulence.

The man began loudly humming to himself, letting the violence rock his body back and forth in his seat.

"I did it for you," said the woman, placing a hand against Maxwell's cheek as the world became a lit powder keg. "I knew I'd be put at the top of the list. There was no time. It was all I could do, and I'm so sorry. I'm so sorry it didn't work. But I had to hope. I had to try. Didn't I?"

"We'll be there soon," was all Maxwell could say. He stared down at the switchblade resting on his lap, avoiding the images flooding in, aware of it all.

"Can't you listen to me? I'm fucking scared, Max. I'm not losing you again—I won't." She slid the ring on her finger. "But there's nothing else I can do."

"I've got my ticket," he answered. "Thank you, Melissa. I wish you hadn't."

The convulsions rushed down through her body in one mighty burst, bringing forth tears; the levees collapsed under the weight of what they both knew. "Please don't say that. What would you have wanted me to do? Just watch? Do nothing?"

"It wouldn't have changed a thing," he said. "Maybe we wouldn't be on the same bus, but they're all going to the same place. How would you have known what was coming, though? I don't blame you. There's nothing to forgive. I just wish you hadn't done it. That's all."

"It's a sin," she whimpered. "It doesn't make sense. You shouldn't be here with me."

"No such thing," Maxwell replied. A wave of calm came over him, as if he'd submerged himself in water. The deafening sounds of the void dissolving around the bus fell away into a church bell ringing—one single, reverberating chime. He was a man strapped to the electric chair, listening to God speak His final word. "It's okay to be scared. It'll be over soon. We're almost there."

The woman glanced down at the switchblade nestled tight inside his fist. "Is that it?"

Maxwell stood, letting his hand slip from her grasp. "I'm gonna go check on the kid." He pointed out the window. "Look."

The world was shifting, returning to a moonlit city street. There were no adjacent buildings, no markers or signs, but they had arrived on the final path home, traveling down the middle of a desolate plane. A gentle bounce shook the bus as the wheels landed upon asphalt. The headlights again began swallowing up the pervasive shadows, burning through the darkness to reveal the empty road ahead.

The woman turned to watch, leaning against the glass to catch any glimpse of what was to come.

Maxwell walked to the back of the bus and sat beside the child and her stuffed rabbit. "Hi," he said. "How's Franklin?"

The child's eyes reflected the fear within himself, and it made him uncomfortable to confront it. He wished for his own stuffed animal, something he could speak to and hide behind.

"He says he wants to go to bed. We wanna go to sleep. We're tired."

"You are asleep," said Maxwell. "Can't you tell?"

"No," the child answered flatly. "How do you know?"

"'Cause. I just know. It's all too silly to not be a dream, don't you think?"

"Maybe."

"What does Franklin think?"

The child leaned into the rabbit's face. "He says, maybe."

"You know what I think? I think you're in your bed right now. Safe and sound. You and Franklin."

The child didn't respond but shifted uncomfortably and curled into the corner beside the window, propping the rabbit between the wall and her head as a pillow.

"You just hang on to Franklin," said Maxwell. "So, that way, he'll wake up with you. And, before you know it, you'll both be right back underneath the covers. Alright?"

"Okay," said the child.

Maxwell stood as the bus rolled to a stop. "You're very brave," he said. "I wish I was as brave as you."

The other passengers rose and lined up in the center aisle. Maxwell reached out for the child, and lifted her to her feet, letting her press against the back of his leg.

The woman glanced behind to lock eyes before gesturing out the window, and then faced forward. Water continued to drip from the frayed ends of her towels and the strands of her hair.

The man stood at the front, humming and swaying, tapping his foot in nervous anticipation.

Maxwell peered through the glass: The building was like an abandoned roadside attraction. With nothing but miles of flat, empty space in every direction, the bonfire spitting orange and red stood like a lighthouse on the edge of a storm. It seemed to serve as a guardian, a violent and wild entity posted between the bus and the entrance to their destination as a final arbiter.

The sight of the flames carried weight, and the heat seeped through the walls and sunk deep inside Maxwell's mind as if it spoke in telepathic tongues. It told him the truth, burning away each mote of debris and dust, until the words filled the empty room like oxygen, screaming, shoving the images before his eyes, screaming, the amnesia melting away, screaming, unable to cling to the shadows disappearing in the blinding glare, the truth like a string of unspeakable obscenities, screaming, until it was all that was left in existence, and the room was consumed by the birth of the brightest star.

Maxwell saw it all. He saw everything.

Acceptance was never a choice.

The bus driver opened the door and walked down the steps. He continued until reaching the edge of the bonfire and turned to face the bus. Backlit by the flames, his face was doused in flickering shadows, and no features or expression existed.

The passengers followed, proceeding in a line towards the building, and stopped short of the driver. He flourished his arm, gesturing to make a circle around the fire. They all took their positions like soldiers carrying out a protocol. The child stayed close to Maxwell, one hand holding the stuffed rabbit close to her chest, and the other clasped in his own.

There were no thoughts to be had, no hesitation towards what was next to come. The voices in the flames beckoned for their release, and all machinations within the group's minds were given freely and cannibalized by the entity. What remained were the emptied rooms bleached and purified by the light of the infant stars now living within.

The building stood before them like an ancient temple, its door the gateway to a dream yet undreamt. It was unremarkable on its own, a simple structure painted by decay, standing by sheer will and stubbornness. There were no windows, no architectural quirks to redeem its appearance; nothing of note but the solid, wooden door that only served as a point of interest for the possibility of what it contained.

But there was something intangible that separated the building from any other structure forgotten by time. A magnetic energy pulsed from the ground beneath it and soaked through its rotting walls. It was as if an entire city lived within it, waiting to come alive when the time was right, holding their breath until the stars returned to the black sky. Waiting for the ceremony to begin.

Maxwell let go of the child's hand and stepped forward, letting the heat of the flames dance across his skin. The driver stood beside him, silent and masked by the night. An odor emanated from the driver, like sterile floors and chemical cleaner. He did not look at Maxwell, nor did any of the passengers. They all stared ahead at the fire, listening to it speak, hearing and accepting its words with no illusions left to obscure the message:

Surrender your tickets.

With the switchblade unsheathed in his hand, Maxwell held it up to the blood-red light. The reflections of the woman, the man, and the child shimmered along the serrated edge like hallucinations seen at the end of a dark hallway. Maxwell cut into the hospital gown, tearing a hole over the center of his chest, and sliced until revealing his entire abdomen. Silence became its own language shared by the group, only perforated by the cracks and pops of the fire growing larger and brighter as if feeding off each passing second.

The flood of recollection clawed to the surface and guided his hand as he stabbed into his breastplate, making a Y-incision. He dug his nails into the carved shape, and pulled from both sides until the bone snapped. His insides lurched forward, the pain spilled out like a howl, and the sutured organs pulsed and flinched in the cold, bleeding and alien to the body they inhabited. They were given, and they were now owed, and there was no time for thought, or for regret, or for remembrance.

All that endured was the ticking of the clock, the ringing of the bell, the monotone note repeating, repeating, repeating, demanding action, as it understood that every second that expired and became the past led to the moment required, the moment that would always be looming, waiting to be called upon, and no amount of fear, nor anxiety, nor numbness to the world would ever slow the coming of the present.

And so, Maxwell stuck the blade into the cavity he'd created, severed the liver from the body, pulled out the organ, and threw it into the flames.

The man in the suit emerged from his trance, stepped away from the fire, and walked towards the abandoned building. The door opened, and he stepped inside.

Maxwell reached into the leaking wound and cut out the remaining kidney, and let it slide from his hand into the flames.

The child stirred, approached Maxwell, handed him the stuffed rabbit, and walked towards the abandoned building. The door opened, and she stepped inside.

The heart began to beat like the war drums of an invading army, and, disregarding the switchblade, he grasped the organ with his free hand and pulled, yanked, screamed, until the sutures tore away from the new blood vessels, and it dislodged from his chest, seeping recycled blood that ran down his wrist, dripping onto the ground. He held out the heart, watching it twitch in his palm like a frightened animal, and hurled it into the flames.

The woman awoke, floated past the bus driver, took off the diamond ring, and slid it onto Maxwell's blood-soaked hand. As the ring left her finger, the flash of recognition faded from her eyes, and she turned and walked towards the abandoned building. The door opened, and she stepped inside.

Maxwell stood alone before the fire, the switchblade and stuffed rabbit clutched in one hand, the ring adorning the other. The driver was beside him, more a shadow than a person. Maxwell turned to look at the shadow, and there were no eyes to see, no mouth to speak. It was an inhuman and unfeeling vacuum.

With the three items, Maxwell approached the closed door. It hummed and the wood was alive. He twisted the knob, but it was locked and wouldn't relent. It told him no.

Please, he said, speaking through the hole in his chest. *Let me through. I came all this way. I don't want to be alone with it.*

The bus driver remained stoic, the flames casting a shadow at its feet that made it appear as large as its presence felt. It was like looking at the galaxies in the reflection of a lake.

Maxwell pounded the door with his fist, panic crawling over the new star inside him like a black fungus, clouding the blank room of his mind. He clutched at the stuffed rabbit, begging for reprieve, his eyes closed, waiting for the nightmare to dissolve and for the door to swing open. He stroked the diamond ring, begging for the brittle memories contained within to float so he could cling to them like a raft in the ocean—but nothing came.

There was only the bus driver and the cackling flames.

There had only ever been one way out. Maxwell knew this and had always known this. He had known this long before he had ever gotten on the bus. Before he'd accepted that one day the bus would arrive. It was imprinted on the stardust that birthed him, that was now enveloping him again, returning to the place from which it came. The ride was over.

Maxwell turned to face the flames, and walked forward, into the bus driver's silhouette. He stopped at the bonfire's edge, and the bus driver was there beside him. It reached out a hand, and Maxwell took hold.

The switchblade dropped first, consumed by the pyre, and the driver squeezed tight, refusing to let go. The rabbit next, swallowed whole and turned to smoke in the light, and the driver's grip grew stronger as the weight of loss threatened to tear Maxwell from the ground.

With his footing regained, Maxwell's hand slipped away from the driver. He pulled the ring off his finger, the diamond imbued with the red and orange glow. Alone, truly alone, Maxwell let it fall into the flames. The heat coaxed out the images trapped inside its beauty, released into the night sky as billowing smoke, and guided the lifeless item into becoming a pile of ashes—indiscernible from the rest.

The driver walked away unacknowledged, got onto the bus, and drove.

When Maxwell pulled his eyes from the fire, the bus was gone. He had completed his end of the deal. There was nothing left but the reward.

Maxwell walked towards the abandoned building, silence becoming him, his hollowed abdomen the proof of a debt paid.

The door opened.

It crawled out from the frame like the tendrils of a living god. Inkblot-black. A shade of obsidian so pure, it extinguished the burning fire and swallowed every molecule of light in the world, until it was as if nothing had ever existed—until the idea of existence itself was impossible to comprehend.

It was the inevitable, intangible center. The source of everything. The canvas of Creation.

Staring back at Maxwell was an endless chasm. Nothing.

All that remained was a single step.

Maxwell leapt.

Terminal Optimism In The Face Of The Event

"How much time do we have?"

"Not long now."

From atop the hill, Mark and James had a clear view of the cosmos. Any other night, the stars would have been swallowed by light pollution, obscured by the kaleidoscope of streetlamps and headlights and lit office spaces, but tonight was special.

Tonight, the buildings and empty highways were submerged beneath the shadow of the valley. The sky was brimming and alive with a million glittering sparks, stitching together the silken, purple anatomy of the Milky Way that stretched across the curvature of the Earth. There was no electricity, no blaring horns, no crying ambulance sirens. Every man, woman, and child had joined in silence to do nothing but watch the evening's event.

"You forget how quiet the world really is," said James. He suckled at his beer until tasting backwash, tossed the bottle onto the grass, and grabbed another from the twelve-pack sitting between the two men.

"The Earth has a sound," Mark answered. "Did you know that?"

"I imagine it's screaming. I would be."

Mark pulled a cigarette out of the carton resting by his foot and placed it between his lips. "It hums. *Mmmmmmm*. Like that. Scientists have been trying to record it since the '50s, but they finally did a few years ago. And that's what they heard—*mmmmmmm*."

"Huh...like a siren song. Luring all the aliens in."

Mark lit the cigarette and dragged until his lungs burned, then responded through the exhaled smoke: "Sure."

"Do you think they're out there?"

"Who?"

James stared off into the sky, as if the evidence was going to present itself at any moment: "Aliens."

"That's a stupid question. You're stupid for asking that question."

"Okay, rude. I'm just asking, man."

"Do you know how big the universe is?"

"Big."

"Yeah, it's big. It's huge." Mark outlined the ghostly cloud of the Milky Way with his cigarette. "There are eight planets orbiting the sun, okay? That's one star."

"What about Pluto?"

"We're not gonna talk about that. Eight planets. One star. We estimate that there are 400 billion stars in this galaxy alone—all in that big purple veil. We're at the very edge of it."

"What is this 'we' shit? You're a mechanic. *You* didn't figure it out."

"The royal 'we', asshole. Us. People. Humanity. You know what I mean. What I'm saying is, with that many stars, it's only logical that there are billions of other planets just in this galaxy. *Billions*. With a 'B', dude. Alright? It's just math that some of those planets could also harbor life. Anyone who thinks otherwise either doesn't understand basic probability or can't fathom the idea that their God created other living things that may be greater than us. It'd be ludicrous not to believe in aliens."

"Okay, Jesus. That's all you had to say."

The men sat in silence for a few minutes, drinking and smoking. The full moon was so yellow that it cast their silhouettes across the grass as if their shadows were alive and sitting beside them. A shooting star flew across the night before burning away in a flash, leaving a blue tail that faded into the horizon.

"And that's the thing about that!"

James whipped out of his trance, spilling his beer onto his jeans. "What? What? What the fuck? What is it?"

"The whole thing with reincarnation, y'know?" Mark threw out his arms like he was addressing a crowd with a grand speech. "IF it's real—and that's a big if—then it's infinitely more likely that, when you die, you're not coming back as a—a fuckin'… moth or something, right? Like, what are the chances that, in an infinite universe, someone born on one planet out of BILLIONS is gonna be reincarnated on THAT SAME FUCKIN' PLANET? The chances of that are... I mean, it's almost impossible! You're WAY more likely to end up some single-celled organism traipsing along some asteroid floating in space, or a 4th-dimensional being on some totally different planet a hundred-million lightyears away, or... You get what I'm saying?"

"Yeah, I get it, man. Have another beer." James reached into the box, bit off the bottlecap, and handed it to Mark. "None of it makes a lot of sense if you start poking holes in it. But at the end of the day, it just...helps people cope. It's all hard enough as it is. Sometimes you just gotta let 'em have that. Especially now."

Mark started to speak but pressed the bottle to his lips.

"It's gotta be soon by now, right?"

"Yeah," said Mark. "Sorry. I didn't mean to touch a nerve."

"You didn't, man, it's fine. Just...read the room, y'know?"

"Yeah. I hear you."

James blew out smoke that dissolved into the light of the North Star. "When did it happen?"

"Like *happened* happened?"

"Yeah. Like *happened* happened."

"I mean, it's gotta have been about 75 years, right?"

"I bet it's gonna be pretty."

"Better be."

"Either way, we're prolly the last generation that'll witness it. That's something, I guess."

"Ah, who knows." Mark brushed the ash from his shirt, staring into the ember of his cigarette like a crystal ball. "People are like cockroaches. We always find a way to keep going."

"I don't know," said James. "That's a nice sentiment, but I wouldn't give us the best odds—y'know, considering..."

"Well, that's the thing: People see what's happening, and they say, 'It's the end of the world,' right? 'We're all gonna die. The planet is doomed.' But that's just that humanistic thinking. It's shortsighted. The planet will be just fine. It's survived way worse than us—hundreds of times over. Sharks, dude? SHARKS? They've survived four mass extinctions. They're old as shit."

"A lot of them are endangered now, though. That's all on us. We're doing what a fuckin' asteroid couldn't."

"Yeah, well. Blame *Jaws*."

"Fucking Steven Spielberg."

"*Fucking* Steven Spielberg."

The two men clinked bottles and drank.

"But my point is," Mark continued, talking around the beer swishing in the back of his throat, "we have this obsession with the end of the world. But really, all we're doing is ending the human race. The Earth will be just fine. It'll heal. It'll keep on humming. Most of the animals, too. I mean, shit, human beings are all descended from one quick little rodent that didn't get itself incinerated with the rest of the dinosaurs. *Life, uh...finds a way.*"

"*Jurassic Park.* Great fuckin' movie... Wasn't that Spielberg?"

Mark furrowed his brow, staring into the grass between his legs. "Shit, you're right. Alright, he gets a point for that."

"Call it even then?"

"Yeah, that's fair."

"I think it comes down to needing to feel important," said James. "It comes down to purpose."

"How do you mean?"

"Well, just about every generation that's ever existed has had some doomsday scare, right? There's always some asshole proclaiming that it's coming to an end on so-and-so date. And it never happens. Until, well—"

"Yeah," Mark cut him off, "I get what you're saying, though. Everybody seems to be secretly hoping for the apocalypse. To get to be the generation that sees the end—the most important event in human history. Like it'll make 'em feel special. Going out with a bang instead of fading into nothing. Forgotten. No one wants that. So, it's comforting in a weird, backwards kinda way."

"If you don't think about it too hard."

"Yeah, but that's not asking much. Here, look at it this way: In general, most mammalian species live for around one to two million years. And that sounds pretty fuckin' long, but when you put into perspective that mammals first showed up like 200,000,000 years ago, it's really not that long at all. Now look at us: Homo Sapiens have been around for about 200,000 years, and just 10,000 years as the drinking, fucking, fighting, non-nomadic humans we'd recognize as ourselves now. That's nothing. That's a blip. If we were really able to take ourselves out completely— like gone, *boom*, extinct—that would be a massive, unheard-of achievement. We're pretty good at killing ourselves—but *that*? I think we'd be giving ourselves a little too much credit. As stupid as we act, we still have that ancient lizard brain. We've got survival hardwired into us. On an evolutionary scale, we're just getting started. We're just big, dumb, stupid babies."

James dragged his cigarette and pulled from the beer bottle. "Where are you getting all these statistics from? You sound like an asshole."

"Google, man. Google." Mark shrugged. "I like to read, sue me."

"Well, I think the sooner, the better."

"What?"

"The sooner we get outta here, the better off everything else will be."

"I don't disagree. Doesn't make it any easier, though."

Wisps of smoke tumbled from James' nose. "No. It doesn't."

"You know what I heard once?" said Mark. "There was this astronaut, and he'd been living up on the ISS for almost a year. He'd gotten so used to the isolation and the gravity change that he got scared when it was time for him to return to Earth. He wanted to stay, but NASA told him, like, 'No, man. You're gonna go crazy up there. Your body can't handle zero gravity for too long, we gotta get ya home. Time to go touch some grass,' y'know? So, he says, 'Fine. I'm not happy about it, but fine, whatever.'

"And he jumps on the shuttle, and it's dropping back down into the planet's atmosphere, and he's feeling gravity again, and the world is coming back into view through the shuttle's window. He starts seeing the ocean and the continents, and then, as he gets closer and closer, he starts seeing civilization. He starts seeing all the cities: the buildings and highways and grid systems—these massive human constructions covering the big, green Earth. And you know what he thinks? He thinks, *Human beings are a cancer. We look like a literal cancer on a living organism, growing and multiplying and brown and gray—this big, ugly growth over the body of the Earth.*

"He's relaying all this to the command center in Houston, and they don't know what the fuck to say. The guy's obviously gone crazy, right? He's just been up there too long. It got to his head. So, they just nod and go *'Blah blah blah, that's right, we'll talk about it when we pick you up from your drop point.'* But this guy ain't havin' it. He says, 'No, you don't understand. Humanity is a FUCKING CANCER, and I don't wanna go back to that.'

"So, you know what he does? He lands at the drop point, somewhere in the middle of the Pacific Ocean, he steps outta the shuttle, strips off all his shit, and just plunges into the water. And just keeps swimming deeper. When the extraction team showed up, he was gone. They never found his body. *Poof.*"

James nipped at the beer before shaking its contents and finishing what was left. "It's like an act of civil disobedience. Fuckin' pointless—but the guy was bold, I'll give him that."

"Yeah," said Mark. "But not just some performative act. The guy was protesting the existence of an entire species. He looked at human beings and said, 'Nope. Not gonna be a part of that. I'm out.' And he fuckin' killed himself. The balls, man."

"Like fuckin' cantaloupes. I couldn't."

"But imagine seeing what he saw. Imagine the level of perspective he got from up there. Seeing the vastness of space, everything beyond, all of this untouched creation, and then coming back down to that tiny, pale blue dot, and looking down at what we'd done to it. Everything we'd been fighting over—killing, robbing, screaming, raping, hating, poisoning for thousands of years—all to help spread this disgusting growth over the surface of one miniscule corner of beauty in the endless beauty of the unknown. How fucking pointless would it all seem to you at that moment? Right? It must have been liberating—that level of insight. Like seeing God or something."

"He saw outside the tunnel vision."

"Exactly. He got a taste of the bigger picture, and he broke out."

"You give in, or you give up." James pulled out two more bottles from the box. "Finish your beer, man. Think it's about time." He pointed to the edge of the sky. The deep blue canvas began dissolving into a bright orange aura, spreading out over the distant horizon like spilled liquid.

Mark drank, tossed the bottle, and popped open the cap on his last drink.

At that moment, a thunderous boom shook the ground like an earthquake, and the orange aura erupted in the sky, burning away the stars like an inorganic sunrise.

"You were right," said Mark, watching the cloud rise out of the otherworldly light. "It's real pretty."

The two men held up their beers, together gazing at the blinding, miles-high wall of fire cascading towards them.

James glanced at his friend. "So. What are we toasting to?"

"To *giving up*," said Mark.

James smirked. "Alright. To *giving up*."

Their bottles clinked, and they drank.

Over the roar of the approaching stampede, Mark grabbed James' arm and spoke: "I hope it doesn't hurt."

James leaned into his body, looking out over the disintegrating city. "It won't."

The Light At The End Of The World

The boy walked through the snow blanketing the empty road, dirtied from ash and debris floating down and around him as if the winter storm had never ceased. He followed the trail of shallow footprints, careful to place his own feet inside each one, retracing the steps of whomever had come before. Every new print he left fit comfortably inside, and the crimson spots like wax seals on a letter fell upon the compressed snow, burning through into the cracked cement, marking the evidence of the boy's own journey separate to that of what could have been the last memento of a dead man's existence.

He likened the blood draining out from his open wound to the breadcrumbs left by the children lost in the woods, the stories his mother would read to him circling around his mind to stave off the intrusive awareness of gnawing pain. They would find him—someone would find him—and he would lead them to the man in combat boots who would, in turn, lead the boy to the destination he believed must be salvation. *An adult would know what to do.* He believed this solely because he did not know what to do, and so this was the only answer.

The road was littered on either side with abandoned cars and the crumbling remains of buildings carved out by mortar fire or Molotov cocktails. For weeks, his family's television played instructive videos of how to construct these instruments of war for citizens to defend their homes. His father and his uncles would return from the store with bottles and bottles of 100-proof vodka, and he'd watch them create their little bombs that they called "poor man's grenades" as they passed around a separate bottle reserved purely for consumption. He would sit on his father's lap in front of the television, its signal cutting off and on as the bombs trembled the walls and shook dust from the ceiling, growing louder and closer. He learned how to make one himself before he ever learned how to ride a bicycle.

After months of absorbing the cacophony of war on the horizon, the silence of the empty road felt foreign and rang inside his ears as he continued. He recognized that total quiet was something to become reacquainted with, as were at first the screams and the whistles of rockets and firearms. His senses operated upon a tightrope of opposing extremes.

The bootprints turned left into an alleyway, and the boy followed along, and found himself at the back entrance of a large cathedral. In lieu of a door there were three planks hastily nailed across the opening. The bottom plank had been broken in two, giving just enough leeway for a grown person to crawl through. The boy turned around, the harsh wind beating into the exposed skin underneath his tattered sweater and observed the trail of blood that led back to the skeleton of his destroyed life. He didn't dare lift his right hand away from his side, the visceral sight of the hole too much to stomach—too real. If he kept pressure, and didn't look, it wasn't real. He could wave away the events of the past few days as only a fleeting, terrible dream, if only he didn't look at the tangible evidence they had left in their wake.

The inner cathedral opened up as he crawled inside and took stock of the new environment. Its towering, domed roof had collapsed in on itself, exposing the wide and sparsely decorated room to the ashen-gray sky. The wind howled like a starved wolf as it passed through punctures in the walls made by flying bullets or fashioned for the barrel of a rifle to poke through from behind the stacks of sandbags piled around the building. Bloodied bandages and empty Kalashnikov magazines littered the floor dressed in a thin film of black debris and snowfall.

Snowy residue still formed pieces of the bootprints, melting away until vanishing at the base of something beautiful. The boy crept closer, careful not to wipe away the man's path, before stopping at the object situated at the center of the room. His mother had played for years, and he would watch her, sitting cross-legged on the parlor room floor, listening to the keys echoing inside the instrument's reflective, black body. She would tell him about the men with funny names who had written these sounds that she played, and she told him music was all that made any sense at the end of a very long day. She told him the funny-named men were no longer alive, but that he could still hear them speak when she pressed her fingers against the ivory. Her piano was a conduit to the deceased. His mother was a mystic, performing wordless séances, communicating with men she'd never met. It was magic. There was no other way for the boy to describe it.

He stepped forward and sat upon the piano's bench with the reverence of a priest approaching the altar, and the aged wood creaked beneath his weight. Though he had watched his mother play many times, he never gathered the courage to learn himself. It was a powerful magic that he felt was beyond his ability or understanding. As his hands hovered over the keys, an idea came to him that struck at the center of his chest, and a bolt of electricity erupted up through his spine, shocking his fading senses back into a state of ecstatic awareness. But before he could enact his plan, a noise like gargling water jerked the boy away from concentration.

Propped against the corner wall like a soiled ragdoll, eclipsed from view behind a stack of sandbags, was a man.

The boy shot to his feet, the piano bench screeching across the floor as he pulled away. A murder of crows flew from their perch upon the splintered high beams, cawing and flapping, and disappeared out through the gaping ceiling. The man's eyes were open, wide and glazed, and dark red blood dribbled from his mouth, staining his black and gray military fatigues. He grasped a pistol close to his chest like a rosary. His eyes followed as the boy approached, but he remained silent. The man's chest heaved with labored breaths. His boots were large and black, and they had led the two to each other.

The flag stitched to the man's uniform was that of the boy's country. It was the first of this flag the boy had seen since watching its removal from the capitol city's square on a television screen. The boy thought to speak something in their native tongue but couldn't find the words. He kneeled before the man and watched the blood bubble out in spurts from between his trembling lips. Without any other response formed, the boy pulled his hand away from the wound in his side, focusing on the man's face, and allowed, for a moment, the blood to drip onto the floor.

The man watched the drops fall, and looked at the hole in the boy's body, and he nodded, the muscles around his jaw straining and forming a knowing grimace.

Me too, the boy seemed to say, and *me too*, was what the man seemed to articulate back.

Words wouldn't change what had happened, and words wouldn't change what was to come, and together, they seemed to understand this.

The man reached out a hand, and the boy took it with his own, enveloped by its size, the skin scabbed and calloused. His armored chest began to convulse, and shallow breaths squeezed out through the blood in little puffs.

The man's grip weakened, and the boy held tighter, as if attempting to transfer any of his strength into the dying man's body. He could see the life in his eyes leaving. It twinkled and drained into the refracting sunlight in the tears sliding down the man's cheek.

I have a plan, the boy wanted to say. *We will both be fine because I have a plan.*

As his hand slipped from the boy's grasp and fell upon the floor, and his tears containing the final light of life dropped from the man's face, a distant rumbling like miles of thunder struck the world outside.

The boy listened but didn't get up, didn't look away, for he knew what made those sounds, but he didn't know what it was like to watch a person leave the earth. It was like watching the shadow of a sunset washing over a green field, a dark but transparent veil blanketing something that retained its beauty.

The sounds of the mechanical storm came closer, and the walls shook after each concussive blast, and birds flew across the collapsed ceiling overhead. The boy approached the piano. The inescapable feeling that he was meddling with something otherworldly paralyzed the boy as he sat before the instrument. It dwarfed him in size, and he was reminded of his feet fitting within the man's bootprints in the snow.

Another explosion released the boy from his stupor, and he held his hands over the keys, letting the blood flow freely from his side. It was warm on his skin and prickled as it ran down his pant leg and onto the floor. His consciousness was becoming muddled, and thoughts ripped loose from his mind, disappearing somewhere behind his blurring vision. The thunder grew and widened beyond the walls of the cathedral, building like the crescendo of an orchestral piece. For the first moment in his short life, the boy understood time to be finite, and he had to make his performance before the end of his tenuous relationship with its existence.

He pressed down on the keys with all his fingers at once, and a harsh, booming *clang* not unlike the sound of the storm rang out and echoed across the open room. With everything left in his ability, the boy tried to picture his mother, and her piano, and the sounds she created to talk to the funny-named men. He spread his fingers wider and pressed down on different keys at separate times. The piano cried out a pained, melancholic noise, the notes yelping and hopping inside the instrument's body, and again the boy tried, placing the image of his mother at the center of his mind. *Can you hear me?* he thought. *Help me find you. Please. Please. Please find me.*

The storm struck over and over, the weight of its onslaught so close, it vibrated inside the boy's chest. Blood dripped from the piano bench like a metronome, like a ticking clock slowly reaching midnight. His eyelids grew heavy, and the ends of his fingers tingled and numbed against the cold ivory keys. *This must be it*, he thought. *The magic. It's happening.* He turned to the man's body slumped against the corner wall, his black boots jutting out, their dirtied soles facing his direction, the steel tips pointing to the exposed sky. *Don't worry. She's coming. She'll take us both. Just hold on for a few more moments.*

Spots formed before his eyes, expanding and melding into a bright light, and the ground vibrated beneath his feet. The boy looked into the gray sky as he played, into the eye of the storm, and saw the clouds dissolve around the light that burned and pulsed with the notes that communicated in a language he'd never spoken. Through the foreign instrument, the boy talked in tongues, an ancient incantation, like Moses parting the Red Sea. The arms of the angels reached out through the light, grasping at the air as the marching apocalypse turned the world to blood and filled the boy's mouth with the acrid taste of burnt flesh.

The great light grew and grew, becoming a tangible force overhead, blinding in its strength, and, still, the boy played the keys, as the skin on his arms sloughed and melted away beneath the doorway he'd opened.

The cathedral walls cracked and fell, and the light poured in like water from a crumbling dam, erupting across every nerve ending, the fire he'd summoned coming to life upon and around him, lifting the boy away from the piano, away from the earth, and into the light of his creation.

In the moment of frozen time, airborne, the angels with their hands out to save him, the boy gazed down at the last tick of the broken clock and saw the man beside him, separated from its failing mechanics, floating forward, leading him towards their saviors' grasps.

The cathedral floor disappeared into a lake of flames, the piano engulfed, and the boy looked away, and, with the last spark of light stopped within his chest, he extended his arm alongside the man, and felt the touch of the angel's hand.

She pulled him into the ethereal plane, and her warmth radiated into his mind, the pain of the earth below ripped out from his being as the final spark ejected from his body. It floated away into the glow of beyond, the final piece of the door, and exploded into a kaleidoscope of images projected across the swirling light that absorbed him.

The images played out for the boy the entirety of his life in fast-forward, every second that led to the angel's hand in his, until time caught up with its very last tick. Like a massive screen in a movie theater, the images conjoined into the present moment, until all that existed was the infinite presence of the angel above pulling him closer into the light's embrace. Upon the screen, her face was made clear, and the boy smiled as the world below sunk into the depths of mankind's Hellfire and reached its end.

"You came," he said.

Flowers Bloom In Bardo

There was another new one today.

The man rose from bed, feeling along the bandages covering his body. The white carnation had bloomed out of his forearm. It squeezed between the layers of wrappings, and the petals stretched towards the rays of gray light peeking through the planks nailed across the window. No matter how many bandages he used, the flowers always poked through. He held the carnation gently between his fingers, stroking the petals, before plucking the stem from his skin. It floated down and joined the others blanketing the floor like a wilting meadow. Some were blue and some were purple, and some were white. But after falling to the floor, they all were black.

In the bathroom, the man picked out another roll of gauze and wrapped it around the open patch of flesh until it was hidden again. A small dot of blood soaked through from where the flower had pierced the skin. It didn't hurt because it must have bloomed while he was resting his eyes. But it never hurt much anyway. He didn't mind.

The house talked sometimes as he walked between rooms. It sighed and moaned, and the floors creaked. But the house wasn't looking for conversation. The man never responded, and this didn't seem to bother the house. It had its own life. It just liked to hum to itself.

Over time, nails protruded from the floorboards, and the man used to pay them mind to avoid the pain, but, after a while, he'd plucked enough flowers from his body that they cushioned the sharp ends. He didn't wrap the gauze around his eyes though, so he could see. Just in case.

Down the stairs was the living room. He must have forgotten to buy furniture. His memory wasn't so good anymore. But the piano was still there. It was dusty but that didn't make it sound any worse. The G chord was still a G chord. There were old photographs that littered the living room floor, and, if it weren't for the piano, he would have avoided the living room. The photographs lay atop the flowers, but the people didn't have faces he recognized. The film must have been faulty. There were blotches like sunspots and the edges were gnarled like someone tried to burn them. He hadn't though.

Sometimes, he would let a few flowers bloom before plucking them all at once, so he could cover the photographs with lilies and marigolds. There must have been a crack somewhere though that was letting in wind because the photographs always came to the surface of the dead garden. The photographs made him uncomfortable. He didn't know why. He didn't know who was in them. He didn't know anyone.

Sometimes a rose would bloom. Not often. But sometimes. They were always different colors. The thorns were painful, but he didn't mind because they were his favorite flower. Once, a rose bloomed from the back of his throat, and there was nothing he could do but wait for it to mature so he could reach the stem without pricking his fingers. If it hadn't been gagging him and cutting his insides, he may have left the rose where it was. It was purple and blood dripped from its petals like dewdrops. That was his favorite flower. That flower, he put in a vase on his bedside table. It felt like a labor of love, picking that flower. The others felt like parasites sometimes. Like he was removing a tick from his skin. But the purple rose felt like giving birth. He was proud of that rose.

He spit up blood for a few days after. There was no gauze that could wrap the wound. But he didn't mind. When the rose wilted and died, he walked outside and placed it on the earth.

The man sat down at the piano, wiping away the lining of dust on the keys, and played a few notes. It was better that the room didn't have furniture. The sounds shimmered and stretched out across the walls. He never learned to play the piano, but he knew what music sounded like. You pressed keys enough times and you began to hear which notes go along with others. It was cold inside the house, and playing the piano made him feel warm. He liked to imagine his fingers dancing across the ivory to the music they created.

Another flower started to bloom from his neck. It felt at first like a worm burrowing to the surface of the skin. The petals exhaled and stroked his ear. He didn't recognize this type of flower. There used to be a mirror in the bathroom where he could admire the flowers, but it wasn't there anymore. He thought there used to be a mirror. Maybe there never was. It didn't matter.

He decided to leave the flower alone for now. He had an audience. It liked the music. As he continued to play, the man wondered if the flower saw what covered the floorboards and recognized what it was looking at. He hoped not. It was best not to think about. *Just keep tapping the keys. It's getting colder. Stay warm.*

Sometimes the man liked to go outside, but not often. It was a lot of work removing the boards from the door, and it wasn't always nice out. Often it was not nice out. It didn't used to be like that. But it was still outside and good to leave the house sometimes.

If the flower hadn't bloomed, he would have stayed inside. The flower had never seen the outside before. He thought it might be good for it to see.

The house always protested when he pried the wood from the doorway, as if he were tearing a ligament from the bone. But it liked when the gray sunlight shined through. Its walls glowed and quieted when the light reached inside. This was the house's answer to the flowers that bloomed from the man's skin. It hurt when it was happening, but the result was worth it for a time. And, like the flowers, it couldn't stay for long. The man liked to think of it that way. The house didn't tell him.

Each day the man stepped outside it was different. He was sure there used to be grass, alive and green. Sometimes it would rain, and the rain was warm when it soaked through his bandages. He never minded. Now there was just dirt. It looked like it was going to rain, but it never rained anymore so he didn't think about it. There used to be a bright yellow sun. He figured it was still there somewhere, but gray clouds covered the sky like they always did now. The flower on his neck breathed and tasted the air. It wasn't much. Not like it used to be. But he hoped the flower still liked what it saw.

On the edge of the property were dense woods. He used to take walks in the woods when it was nicer outside, but, after a few walks, he realized there was no life in the woods but the trees themselves. The trees were dying. Not like how trees turn orange and red before shedding their leaves in the fall. They were wilting like the picked flowers lining the floors of the house. Death wasn't always pretty. It was never pretty anymore.

Just inside the woods was a small clearing. At the center of the clearing was a gravestone. It had been there as long as he could remember. It could have been there for days or weeks or forever. But that part didn't matter. What mattered was that it was there.

The man introduced the flower to the gravestone. It was the only thing worth showing the flower. He sat down upon the lumps of earth and looked at the gravestone. There were no words written on the gravestone. There had never been. But every so often, he'd return to the gravestone to see if any had appeared. It made no sense that this would happen. There was nobody else. It was hope, though. There was hope in places where the unknown existed. That was a nice sentiment, he thought.

He liked to think there was someone buried beneath the earth he sat upon. That there used to be someone else. Even if they were dead, it was less lonely that way. He wondered what the house looked like when the dead person was alive. Or if there was more grass. More sunshine. Rain. He liked to imagine that the dead person lived in the same house, and, when they were alive, so too was the world. He liked to imagine there were animals that ran throughout the woods. Sometimes, he thought it would make him sad to dwell on that possibility. But it didn't. It made him happy to think that the world used to be a nicer place. That it wasn't always like this. That meant one day it could come back. The nice place that it used to be.

The flower on his neck stretched its stem towards the forest canopy. He stroked its petals and plucked it from his skin. Between his fingers, its petals were like velvet or fur. They were shaped like bells, and they were bright red. The man didn't notice the blood that had been drawn. The blood looked like it had always been a part of the flower. He placed the flower at the foot of the gravestone, next to the wilted remains of the rose. It wasn't his favorite flower, but it was new. Its newness felt exciting. Not all change was atrophy. That was a nice thing to know. He decided that was reason enough to leave it outside the house. And besides, everything needed to know it was not alone. Nothing wants to die in isolation.

The man stood to walk back inside the house and bandage his wound. It had not been a bad day.

The man was in a great deal of pain when he awoke the next morning.

The longer time went on, the longer he would allow himself to sleep. It didn't matter how long he slept. Unconsciousness was a blink. It was a brief gap in existence. It had never been anything else. Sometimes, he would awake and force himself back to sleep, knowing by the sighs of the house and the gray light shining through the wooden boards that the world continued to atrophy. Though it had never happened, and somewhere inside he knew it wouldn't, the man still held on to hope that one day he would awake and the world would return to a state long before his memory. Without that hope, there was nothing worth waking up to.

There were at least a dozen of them. Like a bouquet grown from his flesh. A pink orchid bloomed from his abdomen, purple nightshade protruding from his calves and shoulders, black roses erupting from his chest and biceps, their thorns latched to his skin like scared children grasping their parent in a crowd. Red poppies hung from his forehead, obscuring his sight with a film of deep scarlet. He ripped out the poppies, throwing them to the floor as the blood streamed down his face. Black, crusted spots dotted the bandages beneath each new flower like potted soil. One by one, he tore the flowers from his skin. The blood came, more and more like death howls, and he pulled out their petals and ground them between his fingers. Roses' thorns dislodged, taking with them pieces of bandage, unfurling the wrappings. Pockets of pale, weeping flesh revealed themselves, and the man felt naked and cold. Once each flower had been removed, he lay drowning in a bed of crumpled petals like Millais' *Ophelia*.

The man walked to the bathroom and closed the door. He removed the bandages starting with the feet and undressed. When his face was bare, he reached for a new roll of gauze, and began again. He was glad there was no mirror.

Walls and floorboards moaned as the man walked down the stairs to the living room. The house seemed upset, but it wouldn't talk to him. It hummed to itself about its grievances. The blanket of petals had begun turning to black paste beneath his constant footsteps. He sat down at the piano to play and to let his fingers dance to its sounds. The notes felt hollow and out of tune. He hated what he heard. He hated what he'd done. But he continued to tap the keys because the cold was setting in. The cold was so much worse than it was before. And it was all he knew, and it was all he understood. The G chord was still a G chord. The house and the flowers and the cold wouldn't take that away. But as he played the notes, a terrible pain erupted from his fingertips.

Thorns pierced through bandages, sticking out the sides of his fingers like pieces of bone, and something forced its way to the tips as if his veins had come alive, determined to exit the body through his nails. It was like he placed his hands into an open fire and could do nothing but watch as black roses sprouted from each finger. The man, horrified, fell off the piano bench and collapsed atop the floor of wilted flowers. The roses grew until they were as long as the fingers from which they were born. Ten black roses stood sighing and aching for the gray light outside.

The man stared at the growths and the blood that ran down the thorns as if a razor blade had been taken to each appendage. Sometimes things hurt and they were beautiful. Sometimes things could be both. Through the cracks in the boarded windows, he saw the gray light expand into a blinding white that reached the farthest walls of the living room. He pushed his face against the cold wood and looked out into the world.

Something was watching. He saw only the white light, but he felt it watching. Magnetized eyes staring through the leaking walls. The man pried the nails from the blocked door, and he felt such anger. There was so much anger boiling his insides, anger in anticipation for the house to protest and moan. But no sound came. The white light burst through the door the moment it came loose, and the house was bathed.

The house was cleansed. It became quiet.

He opened the door, already recoiling from the cold he was to let in, but it wasn't cold. It wasn't cold at all. The white light shone from just beyond the forest's edge. Growing pains struck different parts of his body like the piano's notes as he approached, and he looked down upon himself to see flowers sprouting. New flowers and familiar flowers: hydrangeas and dianthuses and morning glories and tulips and roses. They inhaled and exhaled in the fresh warmth, and the man's body was the soil for a vivid, phantasmagoric garden. They grew and grew, and they peeled off the layers of bandages adorning his being. And shedding his mummified skin, basking in the fertile heat, the man crossed the treeline into the clearing.

Standing at the foot of the empty gravestone, was a deer. Behind the glowing light it produced, the deer was white and small. Its antlers were two long stalks of foxglove. It wasn't afraid of the man. It stood watching. But the man was afraid. So afraid. There was a reason, but he didn't know how to articulate it. The deer wasn't looking for an answer, anyway. It was just a deer.

A white posy clawed its way to the surface of the man's cheek, and he winced. It was becoming harder to breathe. The deer watched, and the man watched a flower bloom from the deer's snout. And together, the two stood with the empty gravestone between them, cultivating gardens.

A creeping melancholia settled across the man's weeping flesh, and he felt what he wanted to feel for a long time. He didn't know that was what he wanted to feel until this moment. But without another heartbeat, the concept would never have been visible. Without a mirror, the gray light was black and void.

The man stepped across the lumps of earth, over the wilted twin flowers, and reached out to the deer. He watched the droplets of scarlet blood staining its white fur from the flowers that bloomed. And he wanted nothing more than to know the deer wasn't in pain. If it was, if the flowers cut and burned and stung the animal like they did him, then he wanted the deer to know that. He wanted the deer to know they hurt him, too.

The man stroked the deer's fur, weaving his fingers around the flowers, only touching the fur that bled and burned, and the deer stared. More and more flowers bloomed, piercing every inch of the man's flesh. But the man was tired. He was tired of plucking the flowers. So the man sat down upon the foot of the empty gravestone. His breaths were shallow and congested as something beautiful grew inside him. He didn't know why he thought it would be beautiful.

He just knew. There was no other way to see it.

The deer came around the gravestone and laid beside the man, and together their gardens continued to grow. As the deer rested its head on the man's lap, and its body became the planted flowers blanketing the earth, the man felt the weight of fear release through his open mouth.

A bouquet erupted between his teeth. His naked skin became the roots that intertwined beneath the gravestone, and the man dissolved into the flowers that bloomed and bloomed and bloomed.

Until the two lives became the only life that remained.

It only hurts for a second.

This is the terror:
to have emerged
from nothing,
to have a name,
an excruciating inner yearning
for life and self-expression and
with all this
yet to die.

What kind of deity
would create such
a complex and fancy
worm food?

– Ernest Becker,
The Denial of Death

Thanks for reading! Find more transgressive fiction (poetry, novels, and anthologies) at: Outcast-Press.com

Twitter, TikTok & Instagram: @OutcastPress

Facebook.com/OutcastPress1

Amazon, Kindle, Target, Barnes & Nobel, and more!

Email proof of your review to OutcastPress@gmail.com & we'll mail you a free sticker/bookmark!

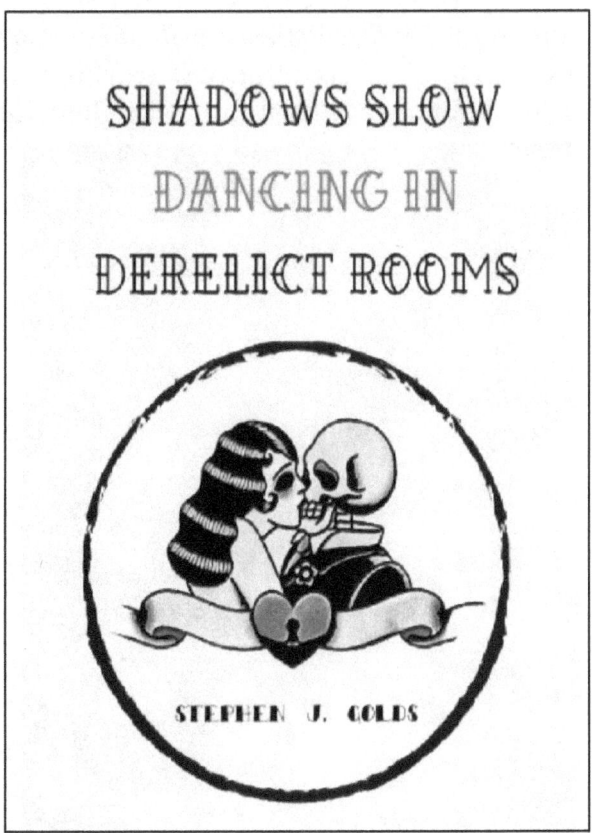

"Raw and smarting as a flesh wound, *Shadows Slow Dancing* simmers with a melancholic ecstasy that lingers long after the last mournful pages have been turned." --Chandler Morrison, author of *#thighgap* and *Dead Inside*

Amelie is dead. Vincent has been committed to a London institution after his failed suicide attempt. There, he refuses treatment, choosing to live in and rewrite the memories of Amelie—trying to save her from the fate he blames himself for.

More From Outcast Press

This collection of 30+ stories is as diverse as the LGBT+ community it supports via The Trevor Project, a suicide prevention charity. Comprised of personal essays, fairy tales, romance, and noir, *Mirrors Reflecting Shadows* shows main characters searching for acceptance in worlds sometimes fantastical but always relatable in its alienation.

Characters include contract killers and CPS investigators, card counters and coke dealers, palace guards and hen wranglers, suicidal sons and conflicted parents, priests and thieves, wizards and roadies—and that's just a flash of what resides in this pivotal looking glass.

About the Author

Instagram: @Jack_Is_Moody

Jack Moody from Portland, Oregon, is a man of many genres and mediums. To name a few: the autofiction *Crooked Smile* about a man overcoming alcohol abuse after a stint in the psych ward, its prequel book of short stories *Dancing to Broken Records* (Beacon Publishing Group), the cosmic horror novel *Children of Apothetae (Translucent Eyes Press)* wherein a group brought together by very different illnesses experiences the apocalypse, and the collection of fiction *The Monotony of Everlasting* (Anxiety Press) about a man trying to undo his immortality.

Moody was a staff writer for *Return Magazine*, *The Bel Esprit Project*, and *Brick Moon Fiction*. His work has also graced *Expat Press*, *Horror Sleaze Trash*, and *The Saturday Evening Post*.